RED

- Recalled Experiences of Death

James Paul Benvenuti, M.D.

RED

- Recalled Experiences of Death

ISBN: 978-1-312-33738-1

About the Author

Doctor James Paul Benvenuti, M.D. is a Board-Certified pediatrician who completed a Fellowship in Pediatric PsychoNeurology at U.C.S.F. Medical Center, and studied adult Neurology at the U.C.L.A. Medical Center, then studied Adult Psychiatry at the Walter Reed Army Medical Center.

For 20 years he was the Staff Psychiatrist at the Glen Roberts Child Study Center - working with the developer of the Roberts-2 analytical assessment of cognition and emotionality.

For the past 30 years Doctor Benvenuti has been a church Lector of the Bible.

Table Of Contents

PROLOGUE:

Fifty years ago, in a U.S. hair product advertisement, lovely British actress, Rula Lenska, begged us: "Don't hate me because I'm, beautiful!" So in a similar vein, I must beg you: "Don't hate me because I'm RED!"

Following the comprehensive study of > 2000 patients who had undergone Near-Death-Experiences (NDE), the New York Academy of Sciences in 2022 published the critical criteria for discerning "RED" - **R**ecalled **E**xperiences of **D**eath: i.e.,

1. These experiences were related to a "clinical death" (e.g., returning to life after cardiac resuscitation);

2. There was an "Out-of-Body" experience of peace or well-being or "transcending the known world";

3. It was a difficult to describe in words experience; i.e. it was "ineffable";

4. It had a *positively transformative impact* on the patient's life thereafter;

5. The event occurred during a severe, life-threatening illness.

6. It did not occur during a different time of *coma-related experience, dream, delirium, or delusion.*[1]

Not all Near Death Experiences include all of these 6 criteria. Some "clinically dead" may not report *any* of them following resuscitation. But *all* criteria are required for the future categorization of the term "**RED**" - those patients with **R**ecalled **E**xperiences of **D**eath.[1]

Nobel Laureate, Neils Bohr, taught us that subatomic particles travel as "waves". Nobel Laureate, Max Planck, coined this particle of energy traveling in waves "*quanta*". Although

Einstein believed "nothing travels faster than the speed of light", other Nobel Laureates such as Schrodinger, Heisenberg, and finally John Stewart Bell proposed that twin particles can be generated and can carry information *immediately and simultaneously - even if separated across the Universe!* Einstein termed this "spooky action at a distance". Quantum physicists named this process *"entanglement"*.

Over the past 70 years that physicists were debating mathematical theories, they were actually *utilizing* quantum (subatomic) physics to develop *quantum computers which required entanglement of twin particles* to give us extremely difficult-to-hack computers which are used by the United States government for *cryptography of our national secrets* and by international banking institutions *to secure our critical financial data.*

Finally, in 2022, Clauser, Aspect, and Zeilinger were awarded the Nobel Prize in Physics for *experimentally* **proving** the concept of entanglement of twin particles.

What keeps this concept from being boring to the average layman is that scientists at Trinity College, Dublin, published in December 2022 studies of 40 patients whose MRI images demonstrated that our ***consciousness*** is an *entangled quantum physical process* - by demonstrating that subatomic/ atomic particles are activated simultaneously both in our brain during consciousness - and *elsewhere* - at a distance from the brain.[2]

This implies that besides our human brain's "conscious life", there can exist "out there in the universe" a "*twin*" of our consciousness. Could this be our immortal soul?

Spitzer's study of the publications of Parnia, *et al*, on Near Death Experiences concluded that these patients showed:

1. An out-of-body experience with an *enhanced conscious memory for one's past life* associated with a recognition of one's death;

2. A "traveling" of this consciousness to a destination - whether here on Earth or to *another worldly domain*;

3. A meaningful and purposeful *review of one's life experiences* - involving a critical analysis of one's actions and intentions and thoughts toward others; with a

4. Perception of being in a *"place that feels like home"*; then a

5. Return back to one's physical life (with one's ordinary memory which was not enhanced). [3]

One patient who was blind all his life, yet when awake, reported hearing and *seeing* a passing train and the streets around the hospital (which was actually occurring during the operation when he was hospitalized and required cardiopulmonary resuscitation for his "clinical death"). Other patients, after resuscitation, reported being with deceased family members and friends during their "clinical deaths". All of these patients reported their periods of "clinical death" to be associated with an *enhanced , vivid memory for their past lives.* Their *waking memory* experience was never so vivid, precise or complete. It was as if their Near Death Experience memories were unusually *enhanced.* A common theme during a NDE separation was "being connected as if by a cord" - yet, "being *above it all*". Spitzer says these Near Death Experiences are proof of the "soul - outside of the body".[4]

From the scientific experiments published so far, is it possible to deduce that each of us may have a "twin consciousness/ soul" "out there in the universe" - which is assisted by all the quarks, gluons, ions, photons, electrons, etc. - which form the invisible jelly that permeates all of space?

Chapter 1: SUFFERING

Although all the information in the Library of Congress (every book ever copyrighted) - plus all internet publications and records of science and literature, now uploaded into Google's data bank (e.g., AI BARD) would require several thousand square feet of "office space" to store it, this data is actually contained "up in the cloud". (Our "twin consciousness" could be up there too).

Except for miracles (which do occasionally happen), all of Creation follows the natural laws of physics. And from the emergence of our first *homo sapiens* (that's us humans), we have passed down the conventional wisdom that if we break these laws, we will suffer. [*Play with fire and you will get burned!*]

And Y-Chromosomal Adam as well as Mitochondrial Eve passed down to descendants a number of mutated chromosomes - which when reproducing statistically falter occasionally and pass on even more faulty chromosomes - producing offspring with problems handling viral and bacterial infections; autoimmunity, and "rheumatoid problems", genetic malformations as well as acquired deformations, etc.   Our biblical forefathers put it this way:

1. Birth labor would be painful;
2. Providing sustenance for our bodies would require "the sweat from our brows";
3. We would *suffer and endure sickness*; and
4. We would die! **[Genesis 3: 16-20]**

From Sacred Scripture written more than 1000 years B.C., we find humankind deciding to blame God - for causing sickness and suffering.   **[Exodus 23: 25][Deuteronomy 7 12; 28: 15-68].**   All hoped and prayed (and slaughtered animals for burnt offerings) that obeying God's laws (as they understood them) and by serving God's purpose (as each had discerned) - would be a prescription for *wellness.* Moses, himself, did promise that a Savior would be raised up "from their own kin". **[Deuteronomy 18: 15].** Later prophets, more precisely promised that this Savior would be a "light to the nations that God's *salvation* may reach to the ends of the Earth". **[Isaiah 49: 1-7]** Many Israelites expected a warrior king saving them from Babylonian or Roman domination: few expected to be saved from "their slavery to sin; meaningless suffering and death" as Christ promised.

Besides the Israelites who felt that suffering and impairments were a punishment for sin, some Greeks such as Sophocles also suggested the same. (see *Oedipus Rex*). Except for some Stoics, most Greeks accepted suffering as "just a part of life".

17

But Plato (a student of Socrates) and Aristotle (a student of Plato for 20 years) suggested that suffering can be *redemptive* - and a *test of character.* [Saint Mother Teresa of Calcutta used to say: "God doesn't want anyone to suffer poverty and homelessness, He wants us *to share our good fortune".*]

When the followers of Jesus asked: "Was this man's blindness (or leprosy or paralysis) caused by *his sin or his parent's sin*"? Jesus responded by saying that neither the man nor his parents sinned but that it was "an opportunity for God's power to be displayed". Jesus then cured these impairments miraculously. [John 9: 2-3] The churches teach that God is always working to bring good out of even the most difficult situations. [Recall the story in Genesis how God put a *mark* on Cain after Cain slew his brother, Abel - so that **although Cain was to be *banished* - no one should harm him.**

The concept of suffering is a common theme in English literature also. Many of the greatest works of English literature explore the different forms of suffering that humans can experience, and the ways in which people *cope* with and *respond to* suffering. Some of the most common forms of suffering depicted in English literature include:

1. Physical suffering: this can include pain, illness and injury. Physical suffering can be caused by a variety of factors including accidents, natural disasters, and war.

2. Mental suffering: this can include emotional pain, anxiety, and depression. Mental suffering can be caused by a variety of factors including personal loss, trauma, and abuse.

3. Spiritual suffering: this can include a
sense of emptiness, despair, and loss of

meaning. Spiritual suffering can be caused by a variety of factors, including religious doubt, existential crisis, and the death of a loved one.

English literature also explores the different ways in which people cope with suffering. Some common coping mechanisms include:

1. **Rebellion**: this involves fighting against the source of suffering. This can be an effective coping mechanism in the short term, but it is not always sustainable in the long term.

2. **Acceptance:** this involves coming to terms with the reality of suffering. This can be a difficult process but it can ultimately lead to a sense of peace and acceptance.

3. **Growth:** this involves using suffering as an opportunity to learn and grow. This can be a challenging process, but it can

ultimately lead to a stronger and more resilient person.

4. **Connection:** this involves finding support from others who have also experienced suffering. This can provide comfort and understanding, and it can help people to feel less alone.

Pope Francis teaches "We are all interconnected and we have a responsibility to help those who are suffering. [*Fratelli tutti*, 2020] "Suffering can serve as a moment of growth in faith and love". [*Lumen fidei*, 2023] He goes on to say: "Suffering reminds us that faith's service to the common good is always one of *hope*". [*Ibid*] And Saint Paul reminds us: "Hope does not disappoint!"

Chapter 2: HOPE:

I s the glass half-full or half-empty? It all depends upon your attitude. In the 16th century, Saint Ignatius of Loyola taught his followers to meditate daily on *both* the positive as well as the negative aspects of each day in order to develop in them an attitude of *equanimity* (a balanced acceptance of the will of God) - together with an awareness of the necessity to *pray for strength* or "grace" to get through the negative aspects. Sometimes the negative aspects or losses we suffer are so severe they lead to hopelessness and even suicidal thinking. Hopelessness and suicidality are symptoms of a treatable *clinical depression - not* examples of "unforgivable sins". Even the churches recognize this fact now. Typically, psychologists and psychiatrists speak of situational depression and major depressive disorders. If a person loses his/her job and the ability to pay the bills, it is common to develop a situational depression which would be expected to be resolved at the prospect of a new job which hopefully might even be better than the old job.

A major depressive disorder is not improved under such improved circumstances. Significant Cognitive- Behavioral therapy and oftentimes medications are required for its improvement. Sometimes, after a series of setbacks, it becomes impossible to "focus on the positive" without therapeutic intervention. And when hopelessness or suicidality is the predominant thought pattern, it is almost always necessary to employ neurotropic medications to restore neurotropic hormones which have been depleted by excessive stress. Suicide is the death of an individual who intended to die when he/she self-inflicted an injury. It has been the 10th leading cause of death throughout the lifespan and has been the 2nd leading cause of death for those aged 10 to 34. Those struggling with their sexual identity have been extremely vulnerable - especially after suffering physical or emotional abuse from an ignorant community when they were the most susceptible to self-loathing. It is significant that on October 22, 2020, CNN reported that Pope Francis declared support for civil unions for same-sex couples. This new attitude from the Catholic Church is a mind-blowing progressive attitude which can lead to the healing of such self-loathing suicidal underpinnings. In the documentary

"**Francesco**", Pope Francis states: "Homosexual people have a right to be in a family. They are children of God and have a right to a family. Nobody should be thrown out or made miserable over it".

But suicidality is prevalent also among the bipolar depressed. These tortured souls often self-medicate with drugs or alcohol to alter their unbearable mental state. In the last decade we witnessed comic genius Robin Williams abandon his wife and children - hanging himself in despair after an alcoholic binge.

And some suffer prolonged *unipolar* depressions with agonizing torture from suicidal torments - seemingly unresponsive to multiple treatments. Recently *Esketamine* inhalation treatment has cleared such severe depressions in only a week or two. So it is critical to find the right psychiatric center for such life-threatening illnesses

Of course, everyone involved needs to help such souls - removing lethal weapons - providing social support - educating them on the new, miraculous therapies - and getting them enrolled into a therapeutic milieu.

Almost all Christian and Judaic faiths teach from the first 5 Books of the Bible, the story from the Book of Job. Job was a continuously good person who had prospered when the Devil was allegedly allowed to tempt him by destroying signs of his success after betting with God that Job would "blaspheme God to his face if he weren't surrounded by so many of God's blessings". One surviving messenger after another arrived at Job's tent to inform him of a series of unfortunate events: e.g. "his animals had been carried off in a raid"; "lightning strikes had killed his sheep (and shepherds)"; "his herdsmen were slain and his camels stolen"; and "a hurricane destroyed many of his tents which were filled with many of his family - who died". Yet after tearing his garment and cutting off his hair, Job cast himself upon the ground and uttered: "Naked I came forth from my mother's womb, and naked I shall go back again. The Lord gave and the Lord has taken away: blessed be the name of the Lord." [1 JB 1:6#22]

There was no blaspheming of the Lord - even with the loss of all God had previously given him. It should come as no surprise that most of the intervening Book of Job is replete with grief - a natural consequence of significant loss. We would have expected a torrent of emotions like a tornado between rage against the elements (even against Almighty God - which we never got), and the anguish for the unfairness of it all - the bargaining to make the pain go away - possibly denial that "it didn't hurt that much" - and eventually, an intrusive depression at the emotional bankruptcy and emptiness because he had invested so much loving energy into his loving family which he so cherished. We did get the abysmal depression of Job throughout that Book but Satan lost the bet. As if, at last, he had his "day in court", Job seemed to ask, after recounting his righteousness, "Why me, Lord?"

Fortunately for all who followed the story to the end, God made up for Job's goodness one-hundred-fold. Elizabeth Kubler-Ross has written of the normal stages of grief when one suffers such loss. She says one typically will amble through denial, anger, bargaining, and depression, before an acceptance. For instance, the death of a loved one challenges our coping mechanisms like nothing else we must face. We often regress and cope as we did in childhood - as if "forgetting" so much maturation we had acquired. Yet once we have "licked our wounds" as we must, it is possible to find mechanisms of survival beyond our last known capacity. We call this "moving forward" with our lives. Carrying the precious memories of them - of the happy times and images of their beaming faces - we are not "letting go" of our loved one but rather we are "moving forward" with all of this in our hearts.

But what if we have been continuously complaining how "bad we feel" to everyone we see (as if it were the flu)?. Moving forward means we examine our full range of feelings. Are we lonely? - even when we are around people ? Is it a comfort to be around others? Are we worried about how will all the chores get done? Is there anyone in our lives who can assist us - without imposing? Are we beating ourselves emotionally? - as if "we should have been a different person to our lost loved one? We can often work through these concerns in a Bereavement Support Group - often provided by the churches or a local mental health center.

Was this "another loss" among our "string of

losses"?   Are we overwhelmed by the losses throughout our life? A lifetime of losses may be helped by psychotherapy or medications. Should we discuss this with our doctor?

Can we openly discuss the emptiness this death has left in our hearts?   (Or is this just another overwhelming emptiness) that may require medications)? When we are continuously anxious with life's worries, we may empty the hormone "norepinephrine" in our brain. When we have poured out our "salve" hormone to soothe our worries, we may deplete this vital "peace hormone" ("serotonin") and we might have to replace these with medications.

We are entitled to be angry that God asks so much of us as human beings. But if all we show is our irritability and rage, we probably need professional help.

Looking back, can we see the gradual healing of our wounds after this devastating assault - losing a loved one? This is normal. If instead, we feel hopelessly stuck in our path of pain, we may need professional help - someone to talk to and help us see the positive steps we have made in our life. Before therapy, we may see the barnyard as an abysmal pile of horse manure. Psychotherapy helps us hope "there must be a pony to ride nearby with all that manure around us".

Can we accept the comfort and support and problem- solving help others want to share with us? Or are we isolating and rejecting the love others want to share with us?

Do we say "Yes, but ..." to all their good suggestions?

Are we aware of the common physical complaints that come and go with normal grief? Or do we feel overcome by chronic pain that seems unbearable? This may require antidepressants.

It is normal to lose some feeling of self-worth with the support of our loved one now gone! Or are we always feeling worthless - this usually signals clinical depression.

Are we having our usual glass of wine or beer now? Watch out if we are seeking daily alcohol or opioids to "drown our pain". Can we work through occasional feelings of hopelessness? We have clinical depression and need professional help if we have persistent despair or suicidal thoughts.

Can we occasionally still experience some joyfulness in our lives – e.g., appreciating God's beautiful earth or the weather around us - or the joyfulness of our grandchildren? We are probably clinically depressed if we have lost all enjoyment in things which used to bring us joy.

In our journey through loss we see our minds attempting to cope with the violent disruption to our relationships and the loss of a loved one. Often our initial response is denial or disbelief. Another early attempt to cope might be isolation or actual withdrawal from the members of our community which are most needed at this time of loss. Like a wounded animal, we want to "lick our wounds". And these are stages of our "normal grief". Psychologists have discovered more mature defensive mechanisms for **coping** against this wound called grief - which may take some time to evolve, however.

Healthy **anticipation** is number one: don't anticipate danger: avoid fearful anticipation: expect joyfulness to come: accept peacefulness when it does arrive - even if only in small bits. "Choose peace over power". Think secure thoughts. Adopt a secure attitude: feelings should be expressed but without a bad temper - (even though anger is a normal reaction to loss). Be "self-led" not "symptom led". You *can* control your *inner* environment. You cannot control your outer environs. Put your mental health *first*.

Humor is number two. It has been described as "your best friend". Be sure to remember some of the "funny times" you had with your loved one -

and don't be afraid to accept the relief of occasional laughter. *Excuse* rather than *accuse*

The Serenity Prayer

God grant me the serenity
To accept the things I cannot change;
Courage to change the things I can;
And wisdom to know the difference.

Living one day at a time;
Enjoying one moment at a time;
Accepting hardships as the pathway to peace;
Taking, as He did, this sinful world
As it is, not as I would have it;
Trusting that He will make all things right
If I surrender to His Will;
So that I may be reasonably happy in this life
And supremely happy with Him
Forever and ever in the next.

Amen.

A prayer attributed to Reinhold Neibuhr (1892-1971)

others who let you down. Develop *objective thinking* rather than *subjective distortions.*

Suppression is number three: it is the brief, voluntary postponement of "falling apart": "work it down, not up". Feelings are facts and should be faced - but there is no crime in "holding it together" to help plan the funeral or guide the children in their loss, for example. (This is not the Freudian "repression" or virtual blindness to the significance of the loss).

Altruism is number four: consciously seeking the good for others - even at one's own risk (for example, those who choose the life of a firefighter). This is a Christlike response that

usually doesn't come early after a devastating loss. Comfort is a **want** *not a need*. Choose long-term growth over short-term relief. Be *group-minded*.

Sublimation is number five: deliberately transforming personal pain into *kindness to others*. This is also something that comes late after a significant loss. Remember that every measure of self-discipline brings a measure a self-respect. *Have the courage to bear discomfort.*

We have learned that the emptiness of loneliness is eventually filled with our willingness to make strong *new* connections with other human beings and to rebuild the bonds of friendship with others as we communicate our many feelings with trusted individuals. But this takes time, of course. Eventually, we learn to even sublimate our pain into compassion and understanding for the suffering of others - which will raise us to a new level of maturity - a new self that brings newfound feelings of satisfaction. We call this level of grief - **Acceptance.**

Depressed people make most of us "nervous" so our instinct is to "try to cheer them up". A person in mourning, however, needs time to resolve a loss and improves gradually when allowed to take the time required for this. During mourning, it may be difficult to "get out of bed", concentrate, answer questions quickly, and to care about daily living activities. Those mourners may be tense and irritable. Even in the presence of others, they may feel very "alone". It seems as if this condition of "shock" will last forever - but they won't be cheered up by someone who can't tolerate their sadness. This appropriate grief at the loss of a loved one does not have to be "stamped out".

Although difficult to endure, the sadness of grief can slow us down and allow us time to take inventory of what remains and assess what really matters as we move forward, regroup, and rebuild our capacities - and make realistic plans for the future.

On the other hand, clinical depression is a group of conditions manifested by long-lasting sadness or excessively deep depression which does not seem to resolve with time or improved living conditions. What differentiates clinical depression from normal grief is the presence of:

(1) **hopelessness** which persists;

(2) **suicidality** which may lead to planning;

(3) **worthlessness** feelings which are chronic;

(4) **guilt** feelings which are chronic;

(5) **"anhedonia"** - the inability to find enjoyment in the usual things which brought joy; and

(6) **intractability** - the inability to improve with usually supportive measures.

The use of antidepressants during grief is somewhat controversial but they should never be withheld in fear the mourner will "miss out on the normal process of grief". Kubler-Ross has commented: "If only that were so!" [5] Grief remains whether on or off antidepressants. Some depressions may require supportive measures, psychotherapy **and** medications. Intractable depressions have recently resolved in *just a few days* with medications such as *Esketamine* inhalation treatment. Many bipolar depressive states have improved on anticonvulsants such as *lamotrigine* maintenance following acute episode treatment with caprazine, lurasidone or

43

lumateperone.   We never consider depression
"hopeless"

Chapter 3:   ELEMENTARY

What a pity that Genesis is the first Book of the Bible. No scientist believes the universe was created in 7 days. And besides, almost 10 billion years existed before the planet Earth was formed - so we couldn't even measure a "day" until Earth had revolved on its axis.

Maybe, the early Bible orators used "day" for "epoch". An epoch is a "period of time or history". The earliest known characters of an alphabet are believed to be those found in an Egyptian desert and date to several millennia before the birth of Christ. (At last a census could be taken and a tax placed on each person).

And then, the writers ("scribes") using clay tablets/papyrus scrolls/animal skins, etc. could write down the oral traditions passed down previously by word-of-mouth from the philosophers ("lovers of wisdom") and prophets ("those who spoke for God"). Tradition dates the origin of genealogy to that period when records could be kept.

Thus Abraham, father of the Israelites/ Christians and Muslims alike, existed some 2 thousand years before Christ – when the story of Genesis could first be told as the family gathered around the fire each night.

It is with such archeological evidence that we must make a sense out of the Hebrew Scriptures ("the Old Testament") written only approximately 1000 years before the birth of Christ. It is believed that the originators of sacred scripture were inspired by God. Yet it is critical that we understand that communication and language is primitive now and was even more primitive at that time. For instance, the Phoenician language alphabet is the forerunner of the modern Latin, Cyrillic, Armenian, Coptic, etc. languages. And the Cyrillic language (like the Russian language) uses words such as "*sorok*" - - - which is to be interpreted in many ways. If the word were shouted, it could mean "4000". If spoken loudly, it could mean "400". Yet in an ordinary conversational tone, it would be interpreted to mean "40".

And our vocabularies change at breakneck speed! According to Global Language Monitor, humans add to our vocabulary so quickly that approximately 5400 new words are created each year! Next, it is critical to bear in mind that until our specific sun attracted our specific Earth to revolve around it - - - there was no year!

Even now, we realize that as our sun "burns out" over the next 15 billion years, the length of time in a day will change! So we must interpret the Book of Genesis (which means "origins") with this in mind.

When the story-tellers spoke two-thousand years before Christ and used the words "day" they most likely were speaking of a "period of time" (such as Jurassic or Paleolithic "period" or Neolithic "period"). We must search deeper for the essence of the passage. The Book of Genesis, first book of the Bible, tells us in essence: Humankind, from the beginning, was created in the image and likeness of God.

If we can trust that a loving GOD created us in His own image, then we can finally deduce the image of GOD by studying the image of man. Humans consist of three aspects: (a) a cognitive aspect: (b) a physical presence and (c) an emotional/ spiritual aspect. Looking closer:

(a) **Cognitive** = the ability to think of ideas; to conceive of concepts such as "freedom", "love", "tolerance", "friendship", "sharing", etc. It is the ability to create images in our minds such as waterfalls, forests, sunsets, oceans, streams, mountains, plains, flowers, people, etc. And it is the power to formulate plans and designs so as to "make happen" these ideas. It is the power to calculate probabilities, envision problems and extrapolate solutions for difficult dilemmas.

(b) **Physical** = our force/ energy or capacity to "make happen": e.g., our red blood cells carry oxygen to all parts of our body; our white blood cells fight infections; our skeletons cover a frame for our muscles to produce movement, etc. and

(c) **Emotional** = the spirituality/ emotionality of the living being: feeling affection; desiring to give love; (willing/ determining or agonizing/ anguishing to sacrifice, if needed; "longing" for union or enjoying the ecstasy of union.

It is possible to conceptualize God "from the beginning" as the primal source of all that exists - - - fluidly speeding some of His pure energy into mass. And it is possible to accept that the spiritual energy of God existed from all eternity as a potential physical presence. And yet when Jesus actually walked the earth He taught us to call God "our Father" ("Abba"/ "Daddy"). God wants us to see His emotional presence – His "soul"/ "spirit" we might say; so we can experience His love or us, His "children".

This past year, the newest United States James Webb Space Telescope was launched to broadcast the very first pictures of the "birth of our universe" - utilizing infrared wavelength photography. [The more distant stars are more"red-shifted" in the light spectrum and so are best recorded with infrared cameras - compared to the closer galaxies of the "blue stars" - easily captured these past years with our Hubble telescope which gave us glorious pictures of our "nearby mature" galaxies.] So now we will hopefully get the Webb broadcasts of the universe's "baby pictures" - which should even be more "darling" than Hubble's.

But why am I so effusive - gushing over "baby pictures of the birth of our universe"? It is because we are finally settling "The Quantum War" between the 2 camps of nuclear physicists - over the origin of the universe - Genesis!

In 1927, a Belgian priest and professor of physics, George Lemaitre, first proposed that the recession of the nearby galaxies could be explained by acknowledging the universe was expanding - as if following an explosion. And he developed a mathematical model with its "constant" which supported what was called "The Big Bang Theory" for the origin of the universe. Two years later, Edwin Hubble, an

American astronomer, perfected the proof of this theory of our expanding universe, with his specific astronomical observations, photographs, and written records. LeMaitre's "Big Bang Theory" gave us the mathematics for the origin of the universe - but it required a "Super- Force" in the first "micro"/nano-second - to ignite the process of creation. Michio Kaku, a Japanese theoretical physicist and best-selling author, developed an alternate theory in the mathematics of "String-Theory" which suggested the universe was one of many universes which intersected like fan-blades - and which "always existed". Such was the talk of our "parallel universes". Stephen Hawking, of the Theory of Everything 2 book and movie fame, felt he perfected String- Theory to accommodate Einstein's Theory of Gravity. He added an "11th dimension" to the parallel universe theory [adding an extra calculus "degree of freedom"] and he called his theory "M -Theory" - which again did not require a "Super- Force" to ignite the creation of all that we can see or measure [and then some]. So for nearly a century we have lived with the "dueling formulae" - the "Hundred Years War of the Quantum/Nuclear Physicists". But which theory correctly explained the origin of the universe best?

In 1964 quantum/particle physics had advanced to such a degree that Peter Higgs, Francois Englert, and 4 other theoretical physicists proposed the mandatory existence of a yet-to-be discovered particle - later named the Higgs Boson. It had to exist to elucidate how never-before utilized primal energy could suddenly transform into mass/ "physical matter" - i.e., bosons, fermions, atoms, molecules, gases, stars and planets - according to Albert Einstein's now famous 1905 Theory of Special Relativity: $E = mc^2$ [Energy is equal to the mass or "matter" when multiplied by the square of the speed of light]. Although scientists referred to this first particle as the Higgs Boson - journalists thereafter referred to it as "the God Particle". It was mathematically determined that the argument between "the Big Bang physicists" and the "String/M Theory" physicists could be settled if we measured the Higgs boson. When Congress failed to appropriate sufficient funds for the Texas particle accelerator, experimental quantum physicists inspired a European multinational corporation called CERN to spend > 8 billion dollars just to build a particle accelerator which spread from France to Geneva, Switzerland and which is called the "Large Hadron Collider" [LHC]. [A "hadron" is a composite of subatomic particles]. If the Higgs boson measured > 140 GeV by the LHC experiments, the mathematical "String/M" Theories" would be supported and one could argue that these multiple, intersecting universes always existed - without the need for a "Super- Force" of energy to ignite it. But it the Higgs boson measured approximately 125 GeV, then the Standard Model of Quantum Physics would prevail - and there would be a need for a "Super-Force" to ignite the "Big Bang".

Scientists at CERN labs in Geneva,

Switzerland, utilizing the LHC have finally been able to accelerate particles and collide them at nearly the speed of light - to manufacture and measure the Higgs Boson - and to "settle the Quantum War".

Chapter 4: SUPERFORCE

strophysicist Ethan Siegel calculated that if the energy-mass at the moment of the "Big Bang" (some 13.75 billion years ago) contained just one additional proton weight, our universe would have collapsed upon itself "in its infancy". And, he continued, if it had contained just one less proton weight, it would have scattered into oblivion before even beginning to "grow its atoms" (let alone its stars and planets)[6] You should therefore appreciate that our existence on this universe is no mere "accident". Albert Einstein is quoted as saying: "Coincidence is God's way of remaining anonymous". Experimental quantum physicists and theoretical/ mathematical physicists offered differing explanations for *"How did the Universe come into existence?"*

In 1927, a Belgian priest and professor of physics, George LeMaitre, first proposed that the recession of the nearby galaxies could be explained by acknowledging the universe was expanding - as if following an explosion. And he developed a mathematical model with its "constant" which supported what he called "The Big Bang Theory" for the origin of the universe.

Two years later, Edwin Hubble, an American astronomer, perfected the proof of this theory of our expanding universe, with his specific astronomical observations, records and photographs. LeMaitre's "Big Bang Theory" gave us the mathematics for the origin of the universe - but *it required a "Super-Force" in the first "micro"/*

nanosecond to ignite the process of creation. [7]

Michio Kaku, a Japanese theoretical physicist and best-selling author, developed an alternate theory in the mathematics of "String-Theory" which suggested the universe was one of many universes which intersected like fan-blades - and which "always existed". Such was the talk of our *"parallel universes"*. Stephen Hawking, of the **"Theory of Everything"** [8] book and movie fame, felt he perfected String-Theory to accommodate Einstein's Theory of Gravity. He added an "11th dimension" to the parallel universe theory [adding an extra calculus "degree of freedom"] and he called his theory "M- Theory" - which again did not require a "Super- Force" to ignite the creation of all that we can see or measure [and then some]. So for nearly a century we have lived with the "dueling formulae" - the "Hundred Years War of the "quantum"/ particle

Physicists". But *which theory correctly explained the origin of the universe best?*

In 1964 quantum/particle physics had advanced to such a degree that Peter Higgs, Francois Englert, and 4 other theoretical physicists proposed the mandatory existence of a yet-to-be discovered particle - later named the Higgs Boson. It had to exist to elucidate how never-before utilized energy could suddenly transform into mass/ "physical matter" [9,10] i.e., bosons, fermions, atoms, molecules, gases, stars and planets - according to Albert Einstein's now famous 1905 Theory of Special Relativity.

Although scientists referred to this first particle as the Higgs Boson - journalists thereafter referred to it as "the God Particle". It was mathematically determined that the argument between "the Big Bang physicists" and the "String/M-Theory" physicists could be settled if we measured the Higgs boson. When Congress failed to appropriate sufficient funds for the Texas particle accelerator, the experimental quantum physicists inspired a European multinational nuclear energy corporation called CERN to spend > 9 billion dollars just to *build* a particle accelerator which spread from France to Geneva, Switzerland and which is called the "Large Hadron Collider" [LHC]. (A "hadron" is a composite of subatomic particles). If the Higgs boson measured > 140 GeV by the LHC experiments, the mathematical "String/M- Theories" would be supported and one could argue that these multiple, intersecting universes always existed - without the need for a "SuperForce" of energy to ignite it.

But if the Higgs boson measured approximately 125 GeV, then the Standard Model of Quantum Physics would prevail - and *there would be a need for a "**Super-Force**" to* ignite the "Big Bang". The debate between the Big-Bang Theory and the String/M-Theory theoretical physicists was *finally settled* by experimental nuclear/quantum physicists in Geneva Switzerland in 2013 by the *actual measurement of the Higgs Boson* (the "God Particle") - which *only fit the mathematics for the Big Bang Theory.* Finally, the 100-Year Quantum War is over! The Higgs Boson weighed approximately 125 GeV. [11,12]

When the Higgs Boson failed to measure >140 GeV, the mathematical String Theory and M-Theory were *not supported by the quantum physics experiments.* [13,14] Hawking and Thomas reconfigured the mathematics to improve some aspects of the Big Bang Theory before Hawking died on March 14, 2018. Being a life-long atheist who thought String/M-Theory proved the "universe always was - therefore it did not require a Creator) - Stephen Hawking died believing in a Creator - just as Albert Einstein (a lifetime agnostic) died believing "there had to be a Supreme Being" who was responsible for such predictability in the universe after he had deduced the mathematics for calculating the speed of light. He is quoted as saying:

> "*My religion consists of a* humble admiration of the illimitable spirit who reveals himself in the slight details we are able to perceive with our frail, feeble minds. That deeply emotional conviction of the

presence of a *superior reasoning power* forms my *idea of God"*. [15]

Chapter 5: SPIRITUALITY

Life on earth involves much suffering, frustration, stress, disappointments, and sometimes even devastation. It should come as no surprise then that our brains are "hard-wired" [through the dopamine system] for reward, pleasure, excitement, and even ecstatic joy [as a primary value or "drive"].

Yet, those of us who seek only continuous reward phenomena [like laboratory rats supplied with an electric pedal] find ourselves *addicted* - whether to food/alcohol/drugs/tobacco/sex/ exercise/video games/gambling - or even "workaholism" - which, of course, results in the very opposite of joyfulness - i.e., withdrawal craving and exhaustion/depression.

Then guilt emerges - feeling "bad" about yourself because of what you have done. And shame sprouts its dirty face - feeling "bad" because of who you are or because others might see your "self ".

Cloninger, *et al.* have written: "For the first time, we describe 3 dimensions of character that mature into adulthood and influence personal and social effectiveness by insight-learning about self- concepts. Self-concepts vary according to the extent to which a person identifies the self as:

(1) An autonomous individual;

(2) An integral part of humanity; and

(3) An integral part of the universe as a whole.

These researchers further elucidated that each aspect of the self-concept corresponds to one of 3 character dimensions which they named:

(1) *Self-Directedness* - requiring the acceptance of responsibility for one's behavior;

(2) *Cooperativeness* - requiring the development of a social conscience; and

(3) *Self-Transcendence* - requiring the ability of one to enlarge one's boundaries - to

(a)"connect with others";

(b) to "connect with nature"; and
(c) to "connect with one's own inner spiritual self ".

The evolution of humankind as a society, most probably *selected* those of our ancestors born with a higher measure of these three *humane* qualities [as Darwin remarked in his **The Origins of Man**].

In 2018 [well before COVID-19 isolation, "Zoom- work", quarantine and fear of socialization and before all churches and houses of worship "closed shop"], a Gallup poll reported that over the past 20 years, the percentage of Americans who reported belonging to a church, synagogue or mosque had dropped to an all-time low - averaging only 50%. It was 73% 50 years previously. Nevertheless, 93% of us endorsed a *sense of spirituality*.

As we mature, we find that our inner spiritual self is designed for something beyond and better than immediate gratification. Rather, that there is a greater satisfaction or "peacefulness" in postponing that immediate pleasure [such as a piece of chocolate cake] - in order to enjoy a greater pleasure in the long-term [such as a nimble, healthier body] and likewise, to the 93% of us who consider ourselves as "having a spiritual nature", I am asking in this book for a serious reflection on the probability that there can exist on earth a greater satisfaction or peacefulness - and even a future joyfulness - which may possibly seem "beyond belief" to many now.

Travis Bradberry, Ph.D., author of **The Emotional Intelligence Appraisal** has given us 18 factors of an "Emotional Quotient" or "high EQ" which he considers certainly as equally important as our "IQ" [Intelligence Quotient] for "success" and peace of mind in this life. He listed these as:

(1) Having a robust "emotional vocabulary" with which we can communicate;

(2) Being interested/ "empathic" with others;

(3) Embracing change readily;

(4) Knowing one's own strengths and weaknesses;

(5) Being a good judge of character;

(6) Being difficult to offend;

(7) Knowing how to say "no" to yourself and others;

(8) "Letting go" of our mistakes [but learning from them];

(9) Giving - while expecting nothing in return;

(10) Not holding grudges;

(11) Neutralizing *toxic people*; [rationally keeping your feelings in check];

(12) Not seeking perfection on earth;

(13) Appreciating what we have;

(14) Taking time to "disconnect"/ recreate;

(15) Limiting caffeine;

(16) Getting enough sleep;

(17) Stopping negative self-talk in its track; and

(18) Not allowing anyone to *limit your joy*; e.g., not allowing criticism to "put you down".

Fully endorsing Bradberry's **Emotional Intelligence 2.0**, the 14th Dalai Llama offered us the "8 Pillars of Joy" in co-authoring **The Book of Joy** with Archbishop Desmond Tutu. They listed:

Generosity;

Gratitude;

Humor;

Humility;

Forgiveness;

Compassion;

Acceptance of things you cannot change; and

Perspective; [reframing frustrations].

In **Normal Minds** , a research of the literature led to the conclusion that a normal person is:

(1) Aware;

(2) Intimate;

(3) Moral;

(4) Responsible;

(5) Self-Controlled;

(6) Self-Confident;

(7) Integrated; and

(8) Capable of maintaining a positive attitude.

[This is easy when it is an inborn temperament trait; otherwise it requires a lifetime of effort]

A thousand years after Buddha brought his philosophy to India, Mazu Daoyi brought the Zen philosophy to China in the 5th Century A.D. He taught that *enlightenment* is achieved through *koan practice* - i.e., meditation on paradoxical riddles - such as: "Does a falling tree in the forrest make a sound if there are no witnesses?"

Zen philosophy is *not* a *theology* -it is not a belief in God. It was Buddha's hope that meditation could *lead to a method of accepting one's suffering with an attitude of indifference.*

In this current book I am asking the reader to explore the spirituality of Jesus Christ. Just *what is the actual* **message** contained in "The Gospel"? As is my nature, I have abstracted the approximately 184,600 words of the "New Testament" into what I believe is the **one** final message of Christ which summarizes His entire public ministry - and which promises *peace!*

Chapter 6:   The MESSIANIC PROPHECIES

East of Eden, in southern Mesopotamia (now Iraq), where the Tigris and Euphrates rivers merge into the Persian Gulf, around 5400 years ago, our ancestors began "writing on cuneiform tablets". For previous centuries they had probably related their legends orally over the nightly firesides until they wrote on papyrus scrolls 1200-300 years before the birth of "the anointed one". These scrolls included legends how suffering and sin came into the world: "The first man ate of the tree of knowledge of good and evil because his wife said "it was OK" - all because she was tempted by the "slithery serpent".

The first prophecy given us was that God promised:

"I will put enmity between you (slithery serpent-Satan) *and the woman* (Mary, mother of Jesus) *and between your seed and her seed* (Jesus) *... you shall strike at his foot;* **he shall bruise your head".**

[Genesis 3:15]

Actually, neuroanatomists describe a core of nuclei within the center of our cranium - called the "rhinencephalon" - the amphibian/animal brain which continuously drives us to aggression, territoriality, sexual activity and hunger.

We needn't blame the Devil for every stray from the "straight and narrow path". But remember that Christ (the anointed one) did remind us that: "I saw Satan fall like lightning from heaven". [Luke 10:18]

Abraham, the father of Christians, Jews as well as Muslims, was promised by God that: *"All nations will be blessed through your seed"*. [Genesis 12: 3; 22:18]. In his old age, his elderly and barren wife, Sarah, gave birth to Jacob (Israel) - who is the patriarch of the 12 tribes of Israel. And Jacob prophesied:

> *"The scepter shall not depart from Judah*
> (one of the 12 tribes) *nor the staff*
> *between his feet, until Shiloh* (Jesus, son
> of Mary) *comes and to him shall be the*
> *obedience of people".* **[Genesis 49:10]**

The prophet Nathan continuously counseled King David who is credited with the prophetic psalm:

> *"I will tell you of the decree of the Lord.*
> *He said to me: 'You are **My Son**; **this day***
> ***I have begotten you.*** Ask of me, and I
> will make the nations your heritage,
>> and the ends of the earth your
>> mission". [Psalm 2: 7-9]

After the Exodus from Egypt and before he died, Moses prophesied the Messiah:

> *"A prophet like me will the Lord, your*
> *God, raise up for you from among your*
> *own kin; to him you shall listen in all*
> *that he may say to you.*

Everyone who does not listen to that prophet will be cut off from the people".
[Deuteronomy 18:15]

Disappointed in how the people were taught by a string of Hebrew leaders, Isaiah promised:

"All your children shall be taught by Me. Great shall be the peace of your children"."***I myself, have chosen to shepherd my people ... like a shepherd, I feed my flock. In my arms, I gather my lambs*** –- *carrying them in my bosom, and leading the ewes with care".* **[Isaiah 40: 10-12]**

Some 700 years before the birth of Christ, the prophet Isaiah was born and became an advisor to the king of Judah, Ahaz (of the House of David). Twelve years before the Assyrian siege of Jerusalem, Isaiah had prophesied this invasion (allegedly to show his power of prophecy). He then prophesied to King Ahaz the coming of the Messiah:

> *"Listen, O house of David! Therefore the Lord, Himself will give you this sign: the virgin shall be with child, and bear a son, and shall name him Emanuel, which means 'God is with us'".* [Isaiah 7:14]

"There shall come forth a shoot from the stump of Jesse, and a branch shall grow out of his roots. And the Spirit of the Lord shall rest upon him, the Spirit of wisdom and understanding, the Spirit of counsel and might, the Spirit of knowledge and the fear of the Lord. And his delight shall be the fear of the Lord".

He shall not judge by what his eyes see or decide by what his ears hear; but with righteousness he shall judge the poor, and decide with equity for the meek of the Earth; and he shall smite the Earth with the rod of his mouth and with the breath of his lips he shall slay the wicked.

Righteousness shall be the girdle of his
waist, and faithfulness the girdle of his
loins. [Isaiah 11: 1-6]

"For unto us a child is born, to us a child
is given, and the government will be
upon his shoulder, and his name will be
called 'Wonderful Counselor, Mighty
God, Everlasting Father, Prince of
Peace'". [Isaiah 9: 6-7]

And later the prophet Zechariah described the Messiah's entry into Jerusalem:

"Rejoice heartily, O daughter Zion,
shout for joy. O daughter Jerusalem!
See, your king shall come to you;
a just savior is he,

meek, and riding on an ass.

He shall banish the chariot

> *from Ephraim,*

> *and the horse from Jerusalem;*

the warrior's bow shall

> *be banished,*

and he shall proclaim peace

> *to the nations.*

His dominion shall be

> *from sea to sea,*

> *and from the River to the ends*

> > *of the earth.* **[Zechariah 9:9-10]**

Behold my servant, whom I uphold, my chosen one in whom my soul delights; I have put my Spirit upon Him; He will bring forth justice to the nations.

He will not cry or lift up his voice, or
make it heard in the street; a bruised
reed he will not break, and a dimly
burning wick he will not quench; he will
faithfully bring forth justice.

He will not fail or be discouraged til he
has established justice in the Earth. And
the coastlands wait for his law. Thus says
God, the Lord who created the heavens
and stretched them out, who spread
forth the Earth and what comes of it,
who gives breath to the people upon it,
and spirit to those who walk in it:

I am the Lord, I have called you in righteousness, I have taken you by the hand and kept you. **I have given you as a covenant to the people; a light to the nations, to open the eyes that are blind, to bring out the prisoners from the dungeon, from the prison those who sit in darkness".** [Isaiah 42: 1-7]

Listen to me O coastlands, and hearken you people from afar. The Lord called me from the womb, from the body of my mother, he named my name. He said to me ' you are my servant Israel, in whom I will be glorified. And now the Lord says, who formed me from the womb to be his servant, to bring Jacob back to him and that Israel might be gathered to him, for I am honored in the eyes of the Lord, and my God has become my strength: he says: 'It is too light a thing that you should be my servant to raise up the tribes of Jacob and to restore the preserved of Israel: **I will give you as a light to the nations that my salvation may reach to the ends of the Earth'".**

Thus says the Lord, **the Redeemer of Israel and His Holy One, to one deeply despised, abhorred by the nations,** *the servant of rulers:*

'Kings shall see and arise princes, and they shall prostrate themselves; because of the Lord who is faithful, the Holy One of Israel ,who has chosen you.'" [Isaiah 49: 1-7]

The prophet Jeremiah also prophesied the coming of the Messiah:

The Righteous Branch of David

*"Behold the days are coming, says the Lord, when I will raise up for David a righteous branch, and he shall reign a king and deal wisely. and shall execute justice and righteousness in the land. In his days **Judah will be saved** and Israel will dwell securely.*

And this is the name he will be called:

'The Lord is our righteousness'".

(Yahweh Tsidkenu)

The word "Jesus" means "Yahweh saves" or "the Lord saves". (In **[Matthew 1:21]** *, the angel Gabriel told Mary to name her son Jesus because "he will save his people from their sins").*

Balek, the ungodly King of Moab, was fearful of Israel's overwhelming military strength and so he paid the prophet Balaam a great price to "curse the Israelites".   The Moabites might have thought Balaam had cursed the Israelites but this was his actual prophecy:

"A star shall come forth from the tribe of Jacob; a scepter shall rise from Israel, and shall crush the forehead of Moab (?Satan) *and tear down all the sons of Sheth* (?evil people). **[Numbers 24:17]**

The prophet Micah (a contemporary of Isaiah) gave us a prophecy of the birthplace of the Messiah/ Savior:

"But you, O Bethlehem Ephrathah, who are little to be among the clans of Judah - from you shall come forth for me -one who is to be ruler in Israel - whose origin is of old, from ancient days; and he shall stand and feed his flock in the strength of the Lord ... He shall be great to the ends of the earth". **[Micah 5: 2-5]**

After the caravan of the 3 astronomical Magi followed Balaam's star to Jerusalem, asked Herod *"where the newborn king was to be born"* and were told it was 5 miles away in Bethlehem, and did not return afterwards as requested by Herod, Herod slew all infants of Bethlehem 2 years old or younger.

Isaiah had prophesied the demise of the Messiah as well:

"Behold my servant shall prosper, he
shall be exalted and lifted up and shall
be very high.

As many were astonished at him - his
appearance was so marred beyond
human semblance, and his form beyond
that of the sons of men - so shall he
startle many nations; kings shall shut
their mouths because of him; for that

which has not been told them they shall see, and that which they have not heard they shall understand." [Isaiah 52:13]

"Therefore I will divide him a portion with the great, and he shall divide spoil with the strong; **because he poured out his soul to death, and was numbered with the transgressors; yet he bore the sins of many and made intercession for the transgressors".** [Isaiah 53: 12]

At the time of the crucifixion of Jesus, while on the cross dying, he recited one of the psalms attributed to King David:

"My God, my God, why have you forsaken me?... All who see me mock at me, they 'make mouths' at me, they wag their heads;

" 'He committed his cause to the Lord,

let him deliver him; let him rescue him,

for he delights in him'; Yea, dogs are

round about me; a company of

evildoers encircle me; **they have pierced**

my hands and feet; they have

numbered all my bones; they stare and

gloat over me; they divide my

garments among them; and cast dice

for my cloak". [Psalm 22: 6-19]

The prophet Nathan who spoke to King David often most likely provided prophecies regarding the resurrection of the Messiah:

"When your days are fulfilled and you

lie down with your fathers, I will raise

up your offspring after you, who shall

come forth from your body, and I will

establish his kingdom. And your house and your kingdom shall be made sure forever before me. Your throne shall be established forever. **[Psalms 2: 7; 1-16]**

Jesus said "It is written the Messiah must suffer and then come into His glory" in Luke 24:46. This is part of a longer passage in which Jesus explains to his disciples that his suffering and death were foretold in the Old Testament. He cites passages from Isaiah 53, Zechariah 9, and Psalm 34 as evidence of this. Jesus's words are a reminder that the Messiah was not just a conquering king, but also a suffering servant. He came to save his people from their sins, and he did this by dying on the cross

Chapter 7:   The MESSAGE

The cliff-dwelling Anasazi from 2000 years ago risked their lives whether bringing supplies or *delivering the message*.

Tyrannical monarchs throughout recorded history are notorious for executing the messenger who brought unwanted news. This true story is documented to be the most egregious execution in history - yet his message was the most vital for all humanity.

M y brother Bob lay dying in his Denver hospital bed. Having less than 25% cardiac function for several years, he had signed up for the U.C.L.A. heart transplant program. But on one of his check-up visits he was told that his blood labs were "troublesome".

"I'll have it checked out when I get back to Denver", he assured his cardiologist".

The blood tests were positive for leukemia! Bob had to undergo a strenuous chemotherapy regimen (which alone could have killed him) - yet he survived it!

Unfortunately, he would be no longer eligible for the transplant protocol. This man bravely accepted his reality and his amazing sense of humor even improved. To look and feel younger, he found some old hair dye his daughter had discarded and he spent the afternoon coloring his hair. Although the dye looked brown from the tube, it dried a carrot orange hue! My wife used to tease him and said he looked like one of the "Sparkle and Farkle" twins we would see on the "**Laugh-In**"show. He took the teasing well.

But his life deteriorated when he aquired *Shingles.* He hadn't been vaccinated for this and he developed painful blisters over one-half of his body. He had always covered it up so only

his wife, Gini, knew what suffering he endured. After several years of this he finally went on pain medications and his heart deteriorated further - he was dying. His son, Bert, told me later he went into his dad's hospital room to ... "have the conversation": i.e., "What is the meaning of life?"

Bert's father was a 64 year-old psychiatrist who raised 3 grown children and had a strong opinion about almost everything - but Bert said: "He never answered my question"! My brother died shortly afterwards and I've wanted to give my answer to Bert's question ever since that conversation.

Many like my wife and myself have suffered "near-death experiences" and often they describe it as a rapid flood of memories from their earliest childhood with a hurling movement of spirit that is "going into the light". So just what is this light?

Yet before we can really consider *the light* and the "meaning of life" it is probably best to start by examining the *"beginning* of life". Scientists date the first evidence of carbon-forms giving evidence of life on earth as early as 4 billion years ago -although the earliest evidence of homo sapiens - our species - can be found only 300,000 years ago. And most anthropological evidence dates from just 60 thousand years ago.

But incidentally, before we examine the "beginning of life" - it is really best to examine "the beginning of everything".

Christ worked many more major miracles than are described in detail in the four Gospels during His 3-year public life. These Gospels also describe [e.g., when He fed thousands with just a few loaves of bread and a few fish] that He had just finished curing the deaf, the blind and the lame who followed him *in droves* all day before the miracle of the feast.

Christ performed miracles "just to get our attention". These miracles were not his actual "message". He told us: *"Believe me - that **I AM** in the Father and the Father in Me: or else, believe Me for the sake of the works* [miracles] *themselves.* [John 14:11]

A stumbling block to his own generation and to generations that followed - is Jesus Christ. After teaching through Moses and the prophets for over a thousand years that God is *one* - the Eternal One shocks the brain and the soul 2 thousand years ago with the mind-boggling revelation that from all eternity, He exists as the eternal energy/ spiritual genius, and "Super-Force" that ignited in micro-seconds "the Big Bang" [i.e., "all of creation"]; and that the potential physical manifestation of His energy existed from all time as well - which he has called His "only begotten Son". Furthermore, that from all eternity, since by the laws of physics He is both spiritual energy as well as potential physical presence - His Son IS!

Saint John in his Gospel opening describes this so eloquently:

> *"In the beginning was the Word, and the Word was with God, and the Word **was***

God. He was in the beginning with God, all things came to be through Him, and without Him, nothing came

*to be. What came to be through Him was **life**; and the life was the **light** of the human race; the light shines in the darkness, and the darkness has not overcome it. And we saw His glory, the glory as of the Father's only Son ... full of grace and truth". [John 1: 1!6; 1: 14! 16]*

Sacred Scripture from Moses through the prophets promised future salvation for the sins of humankind through a Messiah who would be born of the bloodline of the House of David. And we are told that Joseph [step-father to Jesus and a descendant of King David of Israel] had taken Mary, his wife to Bethlehem at the time Jesus was born.

"But you, O Bethlehem Ephrathah,

who are little to be among the clans of

Judah - from you shall come forth for

me one who is to be ruler in Israel -

whose origin is from old, from ancient

days; and he shall stand and feed his

flock in the strength of the Lord ... He

shall be great to the ends of the

earth." [Micah 5:2!5]

And some 700 years before the birth of Christ, the prophet Isaiah [a contemporary of Micah] was born and became an advisor to the king of Judah. Twelve years before the Assyrian siege of Jerusalem, Isaiah had predicted this invasion [allegedly to show his power of prophecy]. He then prophesied to King Ahaz:

> *"Listen, O house of David! Therefore, the Lord, Himself will give you this sign: the virgin shall be with child, and bear a son and shall name him Emanuel, which means 'God is with you'".[Isaiah 7:14]*

The Greek word to describe this virgin-birth was *"parthenos"* and it implies an absence of insemination. Biologists have long known that an external energy [such as a pinprick into a frog's egg] can produce a normal pollywog by a process known as *parthenogenesis*. We must assume if a "Super-Force" was required to ignite "the Big Bang" of creation, that same

"Super-Force" could "spark" a soul into a virgin's egg in order to transform His "potential physical presence" into an actual "begotten Son".

The "birth announcement" of this "begotten Son" appears to be another of God's miraculous events. If you were able to use a computer program such as "Starry Night" - used by many planetariums and university astrophysics departments today - and if you were to program the date to 3 years before the birth of the Christ child [3 B.C. or "b.c.e."] - and also program the geographic area to be the Middle East - you would see an amazing sight. It would be identical to what the 3 magi [scientist-astronomers of that time] would be seeing as they studied the movement of the stars and planets in anticipation of the Messianic Torah prophecies which they were knowledgeable of from Sacred Scriptures of that time.

The planetarium "sky" [ceiling] and the sky over Bethlehem shows the giant planet, Jupiter [considered "divine" by the Roman Empire which thought Jupiter was the "chief God"] - seemingly circling on 3 occasions [actually a retrograde movement which seemed to show a triple "crowning"] of the brightest "Ruler/King" Star named "Regulus". All of this was occurring in the constellation "Leo" [the lion star cluster] . This could have been interpreted by the Magi as "a divine crowning for a King of kings".

The lion was the flag emblem for the tribe of Judah and the Book of Genesis predicted the Messiah would come from the tribe of Judah.

[Genesis 49:2; 8"10]. A later referral to the Messiah from the Book of Revelations reads: "Weep no more; behold the Lion of the tribe of Judah, the Root of David, has conquered." [Revelations 5:1"14]

All of this planetary-star-constellation/ conjunction and seemingly "stable" star over Bethlehem can be reproduced at the Griffith Observatory computerized "sky" in Los Angeles, California as well at other planetariums. This computer program would also certify such a planetary conjunction will not recur before the dissolution of our own planet in 15 billion years. The biblical story might place Christ's actual birth to possibly several years "b.c.e." [The movements of stars and planets are mathematically predictable].[11]

We can assume this awesome conjunction led the 3 magi to travel by caravan to Jerusalem to ask King Herod exactly "where the newborn king of the Jews could be found". Herod's advisors would reveal Bethlehem - a mere 5 miles away - was Micah's prediction for a ruler's birth. So frightening was the prophecy of the Messiah to King Herod that when the Magi failed to return to tell him what they found in Bethlehem [as he had asked them to do] he then massacred all newborn males of Bethlehem 2 years of age or younger. He didn't want any king/Messiah from the house of David threatening *his* dynasty.

And predictably Herod's son, Herod Antipas, would succeed Herod and be instrumental in judging Christ as "treasonous

to Rome" - an "illegitimate King of the Jews".
He thus returned Jesus to Pontius Pilate - the
governor of the Roman province Judea - for
only Rome could appoint kings and [more
importantly] only Rome could crucify Christ. Of
course Jesus told Pilate plainly: *"My kingdom is
not of this world ... were it so, my Father would
send down legions of angels to defend me"*.

The Star of Bethlehem announcing the
birth of Jesus would be just one of God's many
miracles. We are told that when Jesus was
baptized by John the Baptist, "...heaven was
opened and the Holy Spirit descended upon
Him in bodily form like a dove, and a voice
came from heaven; "You are my beloved Son;
with you I am well pleased." [Luke 3:15-16;
21-22]

And later when Jesus went up the mountain to pray with some of His disciples: "Jesus took Peter, James, and John and led them up a high mountain apart by themselves. And he was transfigured before them, and his clothes became dazzling white, such as no fuller on earth could bleach them. Then Elijah appeared to them along with Moses, and they were conversing with Jesus. Then Peter said to Jesus in reply, `Rabbi, it is good that we are here! Let us make three tents: one for you, one for Moses, and one for Elijah.' He hardly knew what to say, they were so terrified. Then a cloud came, casting a shadow over them; from the cloud came a voice, 'This is my beloved Son. Listen to him.' Suddenly, looking around, they no longer saw anyone but Jesus alone with them.

As they were coming down from the mountain, he charged them not to relate what they had seen to anyone, "except when the Son of Man had risen from the dead."

The Gospels Reveal Christ Speaking

In one of his many dialogues with the Jewish people Jesus astonished them by revealing: 'Abraham your father rejoiced to see my day; he saw it and was glad.' So the Jews said to him, 'You are not yet fifty years old and you have seen Abraham?' Jesus said to them : "Amen, amen, I say to you, before Abraham came to be, **I AM**'." Just as God, the Father, revealed himself to Moses as **I AM**, so now Jesus has attempted to reveal to the world that He, had come to earth as the "Son of God".

There had to be a Creative energy for all eternity - who also always existed as a *potential physical presence* for all eternity - the *WORD of God/ the SON of God* - and that Son would have a soul - *the HOLY SPIRIT* of God. This was blasphemy to many in His audience yet God had promised through many of His prophets: "I Myself will shepherd My people". So Jesus said:

"**I AM** THE GOOD SHEPHERD. A good shepherd lays down his life for the sheep. A hired man, who is not a shepherd and whose sheep are not his own, sees a wolf coming and leaves the sheep and runs away. And the wolf catches and scatters them. This is because he works for pay and has no concern for the sheep. **I AM** the good shepherd and I know mine and mine know me, just as the Father knows me and I know the father; and *I will lay* *down my life* for the sheep. I have other sheep that do not belong to this fold. These also I must lead, and they will hear my voice, and there will be one flock, one shepherd. This is why the Father loves me, because I lay down my life in order to take it up again. No one takes it from me, but I lay it down on my own. *I have power to lay it down and power to take it up again.* This command I have received from my Father.

I AM the gate for the sheep. Truly, I say to you, he who does not enter the sheepfold by the gate but climbs in by another way, that man is a thief and a robber, but he who enters by the gate is the shepherd of the sheep. To him, the gatekeeper opens; the sheep hear his voice, and he calls his own sheep by name and leads them out. When he has brought out all his own he goes before them, and the sheep follow him, for they know his voice. A stranger they will not follow, but they will flee from him, for they do not know the voice of strangers. Truly, truly I say to you I AM the gate of the sheep. All who came before me are thieves and robbers; but the sheep did not heed them. I AM the gate; if anyone enters by me, he/she will be saved, and will go in and out and find pasture.

I AM the tree vine, and My Father is the vine- dresser. Every branch of mine that bears no fruit, he takes away, and every branch that does bear fruit he prunes, that it may bear more fruit. You are already made clean by the word which I have spoken to you. Abide in me, and I in you. As the branch cannot bear fruit by itself, unless it abides in the vine, neither can you, unless you abide in Me. I AM the vine, you are the branches. He who abides in me and I in him, he it is that bears much fruit, for apart from me you can do nothing. If a man does not abide in me he is cast forth as a branch and withers; and the branches are gathered, thrown into the fire and burned.

If you abide in me, and my words abide in you, ask whatever you will, and it shall be done for you. By this my Father is glorified, that you bear much fruit, and so prove to be my disciple. As the Father has loved me, so have I loved you; abide in my love. If you keep my commandments you will abide in my love, just as I have kept my Father's commandments and abide in His love.

I AM the light of the world; he who follows me will not walk in darkness but will have the light of life. And this is the judgment that the light has come into the world, and men loved the darkness rather than light because their deeds were evil. For everyone who does evil hates the light, and does not come to the light, lest his deeds should be exposed. But he who does what is true comes to the light that it may be clearly seen that his deeds have been wrought in God. Live in the light. But when you fail in your quest for goodness, ask for forgiveness. While I was preaching my Sermon on the Mount I taught you how to pray: "Our Father who are in heaven, hallowed be Thy name. Thy kingdom come; Thy will be done, on earth as it is in heaven. Give us this day our daily bread; and forgive us our debts, as we also have forgiven our debtors, and lead us not into temptation, but deliver us from evil". For if you forgive men their trespasses, your heavenly father also will forgive you, but if you do not forgive men their trespasses, neither will your Father forgive your trespasses. Recall how the Israelites wouldn't forgive Moses or God who had rescued them from slavery in Egypt but had to lead them into the desert where food and water were scarce!

"From Mount Sinai the children of Israel set out on the Red Sea road, to bypass the land of Edom. But with their patience worn out by the journey, the people complained against God and Moses, 'Why have you brought us up from Egypt to die in this desert, where there is no food or water? We are disgusted with this wretched food." In punishment the LORD sent among people seraph serpents, which bit the people so that many of them died. Then the people came to Moses and said, "We have sinned in complaining against the Lord and you. Pray the Lord to take the serpents away from us." So Moses prayed for the people, and the Lord said to Moses, "Make a seraph and mount it on a pole, and whoever looks at it will live." Moses accordingly made a bronze serpent and mounted it on a pole, and whenever anyone who had been bitten by a serpent looked at the bronze serpent, he lived.

And as Moses lifted up the serpent in the wilderness, so must the Son of Man be lifted up, that whoever believes in him may have eternal life. When you have lifted up the son of Man then you will know that **I AM** He, and that I do nothing on my own authority but speak thus as the Father taught me. For God so loved the world He gave His only Son, that whoever believes in Him should not perish, but have eternal life.

For God sent the Son into the world not to condemn the world, but that the world might be saved through him. But it was for this purpose that I came to this hour. And when **I AM** *lifted up from the earth, I will draw everyone to myself."* (I AM speaking of My Crucifixion).

Whoever keeps my word will never see death. When I said this people thought "For sure, he is possessed". They said, "Abraham died, as did the prophets, yet you say "Whoever keeps my word will never taste death. Are you greater than our father Abraham, who died? Or the prophets, who died? Who do you make yourself out to be?"

I told them, "Abraham, your father, rejoiced to see my day; he saw it and was glad." The people then asked, "You are not yet fifty years old and you have seen Abraham?" I told them, *"Truly I say to you, before Abraham came to be,* **I AM'**."

I AM *the bread of life*; whoever comes to me will never hunger, and whoever believes in me will never thirst . . . I will not reject anyone who comes to me, because I came down from heaven not to do my own will but the will of the One who sent Me. And this is the will of the One who sent me, that I should not lose anything of what He gave me, but that I should raise it on the last day. For this is the will of My Father, that everyone who witnesses the Son and believes in Him may have eternal life, and I shall raise him on the last day.

The crowd said me Me: "What sign can you do, that we may see and believe in you? What can you do? Our ancestors ate manna in the desert, as it is written: "He gave them bread from heaven to eat." So I told them: 'Amen, amen, I say to you, it was not Moses who gave the bread from heaven; my Father gives you the true bread from heaven; for the bread of God is that which comes down from heaven and gives life to the world'. So they said to me: "Sir, give us this bread always." And I told them: '**I AM** *the bread of life; whoever comes to me will never hunger and whoever believes in me will never thirst*'. Your ancestors ate the manna in the desert, but they died; this is the bread that comes down from heaven so that one may eat it and not die. '**I AM** *the living bread that came* *down from heaven; whoever eats this bread will live forever; and the bread that I will give is my flesh for the life of the world'.*

They all quarreled among themselves, saying, "How can this man give us his flesh to eat?" Saint Paul told them about My last supper on earth:"I received from the Lord

what I also handed on to you, that the Lord, Jesus, on the night he was handed over, took bread, and, after he had given thanks, broke it and said:

> *"This is My body that is for you. Do this in remembrance of Me."* In the same way also the cup, after supper saying, *"This cup is the new covenant in My blood. Do this, as often as you drink it, in remembrance of me".*

Christ Invites All

From the first breath we inhaled on earth, we were able to continue to live on this earth. And just as we live without any awareness of the oxygen and air required to sustain us, so too, we can live in the spiritual realm of God without much awareness of the energy/ spirit/ "breath of God" which sustains our spiritual life. But life is so much more *meaningful* when we do become aware.

Christ warned *"Not everyone who says to me, Lord, Lord, will enter the kingdom of heaven, but only the one who does the will of my Father"*. Jesus told Nicodemus: *"Unless one is born of water and the Spirit, one cannot enter the kingdom of God. That which is born of flesh is flesh. And that which is born of spirit is spirit.* [John 3:5#9]

At birth we are born into the physical world and tempted by "worldly things". These can be an extreme distraction at times and, for many, might become the sole purpose of existence. That is not what God intended for us. He wants us to undergo a *spiritual rebirth* - to be born into God's spiritual realm following God's spiritual laws and principles.

This transformation can begin with our baptism of water [or "!re", i.e., suffering for our faith]; or for those who have no other opportunity, with a "baptism of desire" - a virtual choice to enter God's realm - a conscious symbolic "washing clean" the "dirt of the earthly world" and an *acceptance of the message of Christ*. The culmination of this rebirth is a transformation of our soul - incorporating the Holy Spirit of God into our

133

very being - and extruding every element of the "beastly world" within us virtually - if that element tears us from the love and service of God: renouncing our beastly cravings to "rape, pillage, and plunder" - to virtually "take off our sandals" as it were [as God directed Moses at the burning bush] ... for the ground on which we walk henceforth is sacred. Though we shower often since we might "get dirty again" - at the moment of our baptism there is "Camelot" - a perfect way for us to enter what Jesus called "the kingdom of heaven" - [the *realm of Almighty God*].

The churches at the beginning of services offer a further penitential rite for the forgiveness of our sins. And for serious sins such as murder, abortion, adultery, theft, or perjury, e.g., there is private confession offered.

The concept that God, Himself would "walk the earth" among us is like a heroic

story from Greek mythology that "only a child could believe". Perhaps that is why Christ told us: *"Unless we become as little children, we cannot enter the kingdom of heaven".* [Mt 18: 3"5]. It takes a childlike humility as well as a trust and faith to enter God's realm - yet *"The kingdom of God is in the midst of you!"* [Luke 17:21]. Yes, it is here and now!

In the worldly thinking of a salesman who took the name of Erhard and founded Erhard Seminars Training ["EST"], getting "It" meant realizing that the human organism could be *centered* on the "self". Altruism would then become some sort of aberration - to be thinking of the welfare of "others" instead of "the self" always. Of course, there is a middle pathway. Philosophers for millennia have always differentiated the world's pathways or "choices" that each of us have, e.g., between joining the "human race" or the "rat race" - i.e., living a "dog-eat-dog" survival of the fittest existence.

Confucius, 500 years before Christ taught the "Vulcan Mister Spock" message of living for the "good of the many"which is a major theme of Communist China even today. But the application of communism [e.g., in the Soviet U.S.S.R.] better fit George Orwell's book **Animal Farm**. Human weakness overwhelms philosophical altruism so that the animals that overtake the running of the farm are just as deplorable as any despotic monarchs or oligarchy as in Orwell's books [e.g., **1984**].

Psychiatry usually endorses a middle path. Concern for others and guilt when one harms them is *normal* - and in opposition to sociopathy or psychopathy which shows *no* guilt when harming others. Concern for self is also *normal* and it is difficult to negotiate life on earth without *self- assertiveness*! [Aggression is seldom normal except in self-defense]. In his early psychoanalytic tomes Freud wrote of "the Pleasure Principle" and the avoidance of pain "to satisfy biological and psychological needs" - even considering it "the driving force of the *Id*". He later felt there is a Reality Principle which allows delaying gratification for a greater social good: a pleasure postponed if somewhat modulated.

Living for Loving

Christ continues to call all to enter the Kingdom of God - to become more spiritual by becoming more *humane*. Just what does it mean to be "more human and less ruthless"? Jesus told us: *"If you love me, keep my commandments"*. [John 14:15]. *"Whoever has my commandments and keeps them loves Me and therefore will be loved by my Father and* I will love and manifest myself in that person". [John 14:21]

When asked by one of the scribes: "Which is the first of all the commandments?" [There were >600 Mosaic "commandments" by that time - mostly health laws]., Jesus answered:

"The Lord, our God is Lord alone. You shall love the Lord your God with all your heart, with all your soul, with all your mind, and with all your strength. The Second is this: you shall love your neighbor as yourself". [Mk 12:28]

When pressed further by a Jewish lawyer to "define neighbor", Jesus told a story about a Samaritan [despised generally by the Jews as "outsiders"]. After robbers beat a man to near death, having stolen all his goods and leaving him naked in the street, a Levite and a priest crossed the street to avoid him but a "good Samaritan" bound his wounds, gave him sustenance, and paid an innkeeper to look after him. Jesus then asked the lawyer *"Who showed neighborly love?"*

Before ascending into heaven Christ

finalized "keeping His commandments " to a single law: **"Love one another as I have loved you"**. [John 13:31]

The Greek vocabulary clearly uses *"agape"* meaning "altruistic love" -**not** "eros" (romantic love). Christ clearly asks us to even *"Love your enemies: Pray for those who persecute you that you may be children of your heavenly Father"*.

By now we see that love is not a fuzzy, warm emotion or just a "4-letter word" - but it is rather an ***act of the will to show kindness to others*** -even others with whom we may have strong disagreements. Even Saint Paul accepted this final **message** when he defined "love" as "the fulfillment of the law".

"Brothers and sisters: Owe nothing to anyone, except to love one another, for the one who loves

another has fulfilled the law. The commandments, **You shall not commit adultery; you shall not kill; you shall not steal you shall not covet,** and whatever there may be, are summed up in this saying namely, *You shall love your neighbor as yourself.* Love does no evil to the neighbor; hence, love is the fulfillment of the law."

This may sound easy to do but do you realize how difficult this one commandment can be to put into practice? It means, for example, that on Capitol Hill, Senator Mitch McConnell, minority leader of the United States Senate, must *love* Representative Nancy Pelosi, recent Speaker of the House - and *we* must love them both - despite our political differences. I'm sure you can think of numerous stumbling blocks in your own lives as you attempt to "love one another".

In one published study of "love" in **Psychology Today**, the author found 10 traits to be present in "non-romantic" love. There were eight "friendship traits". These are:

1. **Enjoying the company** of one another;

2. **Acceptance** of the other - without trying to "change" the other;

3. **Trusting** - that each will act in each other's best interest;

6. **Confiding** - in one another (assuming the other is trustworthy);

7. **Understanding** - the values of the other; and

8. **Spontaneity** - allowing each other freedom to "be oneself".

9. **Respecting** one another's choices; and

10. **Mutual Assistance** - in times of need.

Additionally, there are two "Caring Traits":

1. **Giving one's utmost** - when the other is in need; sometimes to the point of self-sacrifice; and

2. **Being an advocate** - of the other's interests to help insure the other's success.

So what is the *immediate* reward if we manage to do this on earth? As theologian/ philosopher & author of many books such as **The Chronicles of Narnia,** C.S. Lewis spoke on his BBC radio series during WWII to the soldiers of Britain who were going o to die for democracy [during the Nazi *blitzkreig*]:

*"In religion, as in war and everything
else, comfort is the one thing you
cannot get by looking for it. If you
look for **truth** you may find comfort in
the end."* [16]

And Christ, Himself offered an earthly
reward for obeying His one commandment to
love one another:

*"Peace, I leave with you: **My** peace I
give to you; Not as the world gives do
I give you!"* [John 14: 27#28]

So what is the price of inner peace?
Number one is "forgiving others". Even dying
on the cross in atonement for all the sins of
humankind, Jesus set the example for us of
forgiveness while nailed to the cross and crying

out: *"Father, forgive them for they know not what they do!"*

Christ's peace [*"pax Christi"*] is not negotiating terms of payments for war debts but rather is an internal awareness of well being - that all is well between your spirit and God. This harmonious resonance of "vibrating spirits" is worth the price of forgiving. Our psychiatric mentor used to remind us that many would "rather be mad than sad" - i.e., they *choose* to express rage at every disappointment or frustration. In actuality, forgiveness brings peace - not just between you and the perpetrator -but more importantly, *peacefulness* within ourself.

Forgiving is the greatest gift we can give ourself because no one can give us greater peace than we give to ourself. Who wants to be carrying around a burden of successive, rageful responses to every real and imagined insult and assault?

Travis Bradberry noted the emotionally gifted quickly let go of offenses and "are difficult to offend". Emotionally mature adults find excuses for the peccadilloes of others. However, we have all heard: "Burn me once, shame on thee - burn me twice, shame on me!" Forgiving others doesn't mean putting our heads on the chopping block twice and letting someone cheat us or hurt us a second time or risking violence "over and over".

It is sensible to assess others and assess risks and to safeguard ourselves in the path of sociopaths. A **Playboy Magazine** cartoon once showed a lovely young blond-haired lady speaking to a gray-haired judge on the bench: "Your honor, it was rape, rape, rape, every time he took me out!" - the caption read. No! You don't have to go out with a rapist on a second date.

Forgiveness is an act of the will also - which simply means you refuse to dwell on rage as a victim - you might feel sad that such people instigate such harm and can't learn from their mistakes. You might have been very angry at the perpetrator. Forgiveness doesn't mean letting murderers and thieves "get out of jail free" with your special "Monopoly card". It means letting go of the *vengeance* . Society certainly needs to develop consequences for antisocial behaviors which might possibly teach societal morality such as "don't kill; don't steal; don't perjure; don't rape".

For the past 7 millennia, humans have shown signs of spirituality/ morality. Almost 5000 years ago the ancient Egyptians sought immortality and imagined ethereal judges of our souls would determine whether one had lied, stolen, or murdered in order to pass one's first examination for the right to immortality. [At mummification, a person's heart was weighed to finally discern if "immortality should be assumed"????]

Almost 4000 years ago, Babylonian King Hammurabi carved his 282 laws onto stone "stele" or posts to clarify what was necessary for "righteousness". But more important to posterity and to civilization, 3600 years ago

Abraham had "spoken to God", moved from Ur to Egypt (then Canaan), and spread the monotheistic belief in the one true God, who would be referred to henceforth as *Yahweh* .

And it may be no coincidence that Moses (although Hebrew by birth) grew up as a Prince of Egypt in Pharaoh's own palace and influenced by pharaoh's own priests before he spoke to Yahweh at the burning bush, went up the mountain to contemplate, and came down the mountain with 10 commandments which essentially ordered adoring only the one true God and showing it by "respecting your neighbor" - i.e., don't take the life/ spouse/ goods/ reputation of another human being.

We can let our governments enforce fair laws to ensure "social justice" and "rehabilitation" for infringements of social mores - while still giving ourselves *inner peace* - by "letting go of the grudges".

Mother Teresa of Calcutta, our most recent saintly model of love put things in perspective. First of all, she taught us *"We don't have to go to Calcutta to find people to love - we have them in our own family"*. And in her journal she finally reminded us:

> *"At the moment of death, we will*
> *not be judged according to the*
> *number of good deeds we have done*
> *or diplomas we have received in our*
> *lifetime. We will be judged according*
> *to the love we have put into our work"*.[13]

84

Chapter 8: IMMORTALITY

E. M. Pei may have found some sort of "immortality" through his architectural genius - seen in the Louvre pyramid (shown on the cover of this book and chapter) - as well as in the John F. Kennedy Presidential Library, and numerous others of his developments.

We know that for at least 5000 years, mankind has been concerned with immortality and that Egyptian pharaohs, such as King Djoser, 2600 years before Christ, built his "step pyramid" - consisting of 6 successively smaller *"mastabas"*/ bench-like steps - forming a pyramidal shape - in the unsupported belief that a tomb "pointing towards the heavens" would facilitate his entrance into eternal life. And for the next two thousand years, each great pharaoh sought immortality by building even greater and more refined pyramids - or relied on mummification of their bodies which were placed in elegant sarcophagi - all in hopes of obtaining immortality in the afterlife.

All of this must have seemed lame and superstitious by the time Christ was born. So that by that time, already 50% of God's chosen people - the Sadducees - had lost belief in eternal life. (Only the Pharisees continued to believe in immortality). The ancestors of these Hebrew people had lived as slaves in Egypt for centuries and had certainly been exposed to the Egyptian culture of of immortality.

The Greeks along with the Egyptians believed that heroic figures (such as Achilles) would live as immortals with Zeus).

It may have been no coincidence that Christ was born 2000 years ago, was labeled a "blasphemer" by His own people who dragged him to the Governor of Judea, Pontius Pilate, to be condemned to death by crucifixion - for the "crime of treason against Rome" - being labeled "the King of the Jews" (though making it clear His kingdom was not of this world).

Because it was after Christ's death was *certified* (a Roman soldier/ "centurion" even piercing His heart with a lance before allowing Christ to be removed from the cross) - and after Christ had *resurrected* on the 3rd day; and *appeared* to >500 people over the following 40 days before ascending into heaven - that religious teaching has *always included the immortality of our souls.*

After raising many from death - to show God's power over death - Christ made it clear to all of us when he spoke to Martha, the sister of Lazarus (who had been dead for 3 days): *"I am the resurrection and the life; he who believes in me, though he die, **yet shall he live**: and* whoever lives and believes in me *shall never die"*.

For centuries, the Shroud of Turin, stored in a chapel in Italy, is believed by the faithful to be the burial cloth of Christ. It is a 14-5" X 3'-7" cloth of a fine linen weave seen in 1st century burial cloths.

In 1898, black and white "negative" of the sepia image on the shroud, clearly revealed an "X-RAY-like" "positive" image of an almost 6-foot tall male, who had been crucified, and whose head bore a "crown of thorns", and who had been beaten with a Roman-type whip approximately 40 times (each strike tore 3 pieces of flesh with such a whip). All of this evidence on the shroud comports with the scriptural crucifixion of Christ.

In 1978 the Jet Propulsion Laboratory of

Pasadena, California convinced the church to allow scientific examination as the Shroud of Turin Research Project (S.T.R.P.). Top scientists included: Don Lynn, Director of Digital Imaging for NASA, as well as Kevin Moran, Optics Specialist, utilizing the VP-8 Image analyzer, which they recently deployed on the planet Mars Soft-Landing Viking Project. Of special interest, thermochemical engineer, Raymond N. Rogers, working with chemists at the Los Alamos Scientific Laboratory in New Mexico - all of whom determined the burial shroud appeared to be an authentic, linen cloth, woven in a 1st century weave of the Hebrew burial culture, with pollens found in the Spring in Jerusalem. Barry Schwartz was the photographic analyst for the S.T.R.P. team.

Optics specialist, Kevin Moran, demonstrated the shroud was 3-Dimensional (like a hologram); that the image had to be formed while the cloth was draped over a 3-dimensional object. (Subsequent artificial-intelligence algorithms have reproduced the entire shroud into a 3-dimensional figure).

The S.T.R.P. concluded: (1) there is an image of a crucified man, which showed only blood at the head ("crown of thorns"); body (Roman flagrum lashings); right 5th ribcage (Roman *lancea*/ short javelin piercing); wrist and feet (nail piercings); and (2) there is **no** paint, dye, or scorch which forms the image on the shroud. (Scorch markings forming a pattern on the edge of the shroud, were the result of burns on the folds of the shroud then

159

which was in a metal box); and (3) there is *no known mechanism on earth which can account for this shroud's existence.* [17]

A different scientific laboratory in 1988 was used for radiocarbon dating of the shroud utilizing sample cloth taken from "the edges". The samples dated between 1262 and 1353 c.e.. However, Raymond N. Rogers, the original S.T.R.P. team thermochemical engineer had doubts and referred one of the sample pieces to the Los Alamos National Laboratory for analysis where it was determined the *samples were filled with* **cotton fibers** **which had been dyed** *to look like the linen* in the shroud.

Before he died, Raymond Rogers testified that the Shroud of Turin contained **100% linen** with **no cotton** and it contained **zero dye,**

zero paint, and **no scorch in the image**. This was published in a scientifically rigorous journal in 2005. Rogers conclusion was *the sample used for radiocarbon dating of the shroud is invalid* - (possibly taken from a medieval patch woven on the backing of the shroud).[18]

Subsequent datings of the Shroud of Turin are consistent with at the scriptural date of the burial of Christ. (See Guilio Fanti's Fourier Transformed Infrared Specroscopy Test; & Ramen Laser Spectroscopy Test; see also Rogers Vanillin aging Test).[19]

Additional electron microscopic testing has revealed both eyes of the shroud had been covered with coins minted in 29 c.e., depicting images of Pontius Pilate, the Roman Governor of Judea. Only 5 such coins can be found on earth even today.[20]

Finally, ENEA (the "Atomic Energy Commission of Italy) calculated it would take 34 thousand billion watts of Vacuum UltraViolet laser light radiation to manufacture the shroud of Turin. *No such machine exists on Earth to this day!* [21]

The faithful believe Christ left us a 3-Dimensional hologram of His resurrection - to give us the **hope of immortality** - to show us there is life after death!

At death, we will be entering an energy field where souls/ spirits/ pure "forces" dwell. Some physicists have named a fifth energy field *"Quintessence"*. In 1998 two international teams of astrophysicists (one of which was headed by American astronomer Adam Riess) described what they termed "dark energy" (and which others have since labeled "transparent energy") - which constitutes 69.4 percent of our universe. (Only 4 to 5 percent of our universe is the stuff of which our bodies, planets and stars are made of). And 25 percent of the universe is dark or transparent matter according to the "standard cosmological model".

This energy field is called "dark" or "transparent" because it does not react with our ordinary triggers such as x-rays - but it exists by all methods of measurements and calculations. We know now that even the Higgs Boson (termed the "God Particle") exists and can be measured by pushing protons or ions to near the speed of light utilizing the Cern Large Hadron Collider (giving it a mass of 125 Gev) although it can seemingly "disappear" into other subatomic particles at other times. And through the mathematical genius of theoretical physicist Albert Einstein, we have long known that energy and mass (physical "matter") are *interchangeable*. Energy becomes "mass" when it slows below the speed of light.

Then, can you imagine the "heavenly spirits or souls" traveling in the transparent zone at the speed of light? We call these angels and "saints" - those souls who have passed into the kingdom of God known as "Paradise". Astrophysicists have calculated there are 200 billion *galaxies* in our observable universe (as revealed by Hubble's Ultra Deep Field observations, for instance).

And by observing the Cosmic Microwave Background radiation (the "ground-glass sparkling noise on our original television sets when TV broadcasting ceased each night 70 years ago) - we believe an equal number of galaxies exist in our *non- observable* universe.

Now, assuming an average of 100 billion stars exist in each galaxy, that means that well over a billion trillion stars exist in our observable universe alone. And since our own Milky Way Galaxy is presumed to have between 800 billion and 3.2 trillion planets (though some galaxies are calculated to have as many as 8 trillion planets) - you should realize that as a "tourist saint" *you could spend an eternity just visiting and re-visiting "your favorite planets.*

So, eternity in Paradise should never get "boring". Most of us would like to "celebrate with our friends and relatives" in continuous parties - when we get to Paradise. And we haven't yet even let you consider "getting to know God". This is equivalent to getting to know one's creator, the love of the

one who died for our salvation, the wisdom of the one who kept us holy enough to "get to Paradise". Even if we have no eyes at first entrance into paradise, *we will know God* - somewhat as a blind person "knows" people and the surroundings about - only even better. Our "twin consciousness" has some knowledge of God which we learned while we were on Earth.

Recall how you can know a personal friend through loving remembrances, current experiences, and persistent communication. In Chapter 10 we describe God as the all-encompassing *Array* of all that is - an almighty energy force/ spiritual entity; with continuous capacity to be physically present as His only *begotten* Son - a condensed yet separate "always-potentially-physical-Me" that can take the form of man - and a force/spirit that can generate waves to communicate - whether through the glorified bodily senses (after the "end of time") or through such "resonance receptors by which consciousness comprehends" - through which the angels and saints communicate. (Just recall that muon waves "tell us" just where the burial chambers of the pyramids are and "read stone" - like x-rays "read our body's bones").

Chapter 9:   IMAGINE

We must admit that life in the twenty-first century has become extremely stressful - whether because of anxiety over an early death through pandemic infection, loss of work through stringent public health measures, loss of funds for food, rent or mortgages, etc., or xenophobia that "The next person I talk to could give me COVID-19", etc. And more recently - worries over inflation, "the war", and housing shortages.

Almost everything that happens follows the laws of physics - even what we call "karma" - what I do has a psychological effect on others and that will produce a psychological response from them. (This might be one way hubris ("cosmic arrogance") brings its own downfall). The exceptions to the laws of physics are called miracles. We can pray for them because some events do break the laws of physics.

Especially because of Covid-19, in some surveys, one-third of the population experiences loneliness. This painful emotion may peak at age 35 but is present at every age. Holiday time may especially be the loneliest of all times with memories of who used to comfort and communicate with us but no longer can -

and awareness that others could comfort and communicate with us but no longer do. When, through no circumstances of your own doing, it becomes impossible for you to connect and relate to a trustworthy soul in your ambient surroundings or telephonic addresses - so that you can share emotions and experiences - then label this solitude an opportunity to connect to God - your Creator, Redeemer, and sanctifier. Jesus has taught us that "Eye has not seen, nor has ear heard, nor has it entered into the mind of man what God has prepared in paradise for those who love Him". So we are entitled to imagine just what is ahead for us in Paradise.

At death, we will be entering an energy field where souls/ spirits/ "pure energy" dwells. Some physicists have named a force "Quintessence". In 1998 two international teams of astro- physicists (one of which was headed by American astronomer Adam Riess) described what they termed "dark energy" (and which others have since labeled "transparent energy") - which constitutes 69.4 percent of our universe. (Only 4 to 5 percent of our universe is the stuff of which our bodies, planets and stars are made of). And 25 percent of the universe is dark or transparent matter according to the "standard cosmological model". This energy field is called "dark" or "transparent" because it does not react with our ordinary triggers such as x- rays - but it exists by all methods of measurements and calculations. We know now that even the Higgs Boson (termed the "God Particle") exists and can be measured by pushing protons or ions to near the speed of light utilizing the CERN Large Hadron Collider (giving it a mass of 125 Gev) although it can seemingly "disappear" for microseconds into "the invisible jelly of space-time" over the entire universe at other moments. And through the mathematical genius of theoretical physicist Albert Einstein, we have long known that energy and mass (physical "matter") are interchangeable. Energy becomes "mass" when it slows below the speed of light.

As incomprehensible as the "Array" of God remains, it should come as no surprise that Jesus taught us: "If you have seen me, you have seen the Father". Two thousand years ago, we "saw" Jesus. He was born in a stable, a humble person of humble birth; with a humble but holy human mother and step-father. He was an obedient child who became a working "carpenter" or builder before becoming a gifted teacher - who taught us everything we need to know to get to our destination - Paradise. Jesus condensed all commandments into his final message: "Love one another - as I have loved you". He taught us to love the lowly, the disabled, the poor, the outcasts demoralized, or "disenfranchised" - for "theirs is the kingdom of Heaven".

Jesus was willing to die an excruciating death of crucifixion in atonement for our sins: we no longer need to sacrifice animals or "first fruits". And with his dying breath, he uttered: "Father, forgive them for they know not what they are doing" - thinking the best of us as we had just yelled at Pontius Pilate: "His blood be upon us and children". When we know God, we will know love and compassion - as we have never before known it. So even before our final judgment, we have "seen" Jesus - and therefore we have "seen" the Father. And we have also heard the warning Jesus gave us: "Strive to enter by the narrow door. For many, I tell you, will seek to enter and will not be able".

Just what is this "narrow door"? Jesus himself tells us that following His resurrection he will "come into His glory" and that all nations will assemble before Him, seated on His throne, surrounded by angels. He tells us He will then separate all of us into two groups: those on His right will hear Him say: "Come you who are blessed by my Father and inherit the kingdom prepared for you from the foundation of the world. For I was hungry and you gave me food, thirsty and you gave me drink, a stranger and you welcomed me, naked and you clothed me, ill and you cared for me, in prison and you visited me".

Jesus continues, the righteous will ask when did they do all these things for Him. He will answer: "Whenever you did these things for one of My least brothers or sisters, you did it for Me".

This may sound daunting on first reading. My personal belief is that no one can do "all that" except the late Saint Mother Theresa. So is it possible our merciful Lord will take into account that "feeding and giving drink to the hungry and thirsty" is nurturing our children or students (or parents when they are old) and giving money to our favorite charities or church; and that caring for the ill is taking care of our sick relatives/friends who are in need. And we can give our old clothes to the Salvation

Army or to the Saint Vincent de Paul Society to "clothe the naked". We can vote for candidates who will make sure social services cares for those in need and provides programs that will be fair to immigrants. This is certainly something to **think about!**

Chapter 10: GENESIS

I **am** the Super Force that created all forces - - - whether you call it the strong or the weak nuclear force, the electromagnetic or the gravitational force, or even your elusive quintessence force accelerating the expansion of your universe - - - whether through your 68.3% dark/transparent energy - - - or your light, **I am.**

As Nobel laureate, Leon Lederman explains:

"The physicists are revealing for the first time, hitherto unseen, mysterious, and ultimate powers, *the forces of nature,* forces that have sculpted the entire universe in all things from galaxies to stars, humans to DNA, atoms to quarks."[22]

Evening came and morning followed, The First Epoch (which began 13.7 billion years ago. Or as Neil de Grasse Tyson Wrote: *"In the beginning, nearly* fourteen billion years ago, all the *space and all the energy of the known universe was contained in a volume less than one trillionth the size of the period that ends this sentence".*[23]

And SPACE.COM explains:

"The universe was born with the Big Bang as an unimaginably hot dense *point*.   When the universe was just 10^{-34} of a second or so old - that is a hundredth of a billionth of a second in age - - - it experienced an incredible burst of expansion, known as *inflation*, in which

space, itself, expanded faster than the speed of light. During this period, the universe doubled in size at least 90 times, going from subatomic sized to golf-ball sized, almost simultaneously."
..."According to NASA, after inflation, the growth of the universe continued but at a slower rate. As space expanded, the universe cooled and *matter formed.*[24]

Before your Plank Radiation Era 13.7 billion years ago, **I am**. Albert Einstein showed you mathematically in his Theory of Special Relativity. You have known for a century that energy can convert into matter ("mass") just as matter can explode back into energy. When some of My energy passed through My Higgs Field *I created* Boson. It was the beginning of my Matter Era 13.65 billion years ago.

I am the MASS, that created all matter - - - **I** have always had a potential **physical presence** and **I** always will.

In the beginning, when **I created** the heavens and the earth - - - the earth was without form or shape, with darkness over the abyss - - - and **a** *mighty wind* swept over the waters.

My Higgs Field covers the entire universe, and is ridden by particles like my Higgs Boson (which you have dubbed "the **GOD** particle"). This boson gives measurable *mass* to other particles - - - such as electrons. An electron generates an electric field that exerts an attractive force on a particle with a positive charge, such as a proton. And as with all particles, electrons act as **waves**.

Then **I said** *"Let there be light, and there was light"*. My Higgs boson decays rapidly into other particles - - - such as photons. These photons travel in waves over the universe. This is My light.

Then a blinding light pierces the darkness of the abyss - - - gases spiraling and cascading explosively outwards - - - drifting expansively. As the gaseous mass-energy plasma expands and cools, *matter is created*. More than 13 billion years ago, *time splashes mass into space* - - - into the stars and planets, the galaxies of your universe - - - spawning a series of stars and planets from which your very own sun and earth evolved. Your scientists accept this streaming of energy into physical matter as the probable evolution of your universe and it is commonly known as "the Big Bang Theory". But each phase of creation required hundreds of millions of your "years". Yet, there can be no "year", nor is there a "day", nor even an "hour". You humans defined time on earth by the movement of the earth about the sun and this constellation was only recently formed.

Albert Einstein showed you a century ago that "time" should be named "space-time" (giving your local coordinates in space and local time) because like energy-mass, time is relative to space. Carlo Rovelli explains how at the *horizon* edge of a black hole, *time stands still!* He goes on to explain how Einstein showed mathematically that what you observe on a distant planet such as Proxima b, - whether in radio communications or telescope – occurred "four years ago".[26]

So *I said:* "Let Us make human beings in O*ur* image, after *Our* Likeness. Let them have dominion over the fish of the sea, the birds of the air, the tame animals, all the wild animals, and all the creatures that crawl on the earth. **I created** humankind in *Our Image.* " *In the Image of God I created them.*"

Then **I said:** let the earth bring forth every kind of living creature - - - and **I saw** that it was good.   Living creatures included hominids millions of years ago.   Charles Darwin, after studying The **Origin of Species** then detailed evolution and the **Descent of Man**.

"In regard to bodily size or strength, we do not know whether man is descended from some small species, like the chimpanzee, or from one as powerful as the gorilla; and, therefore we cannot say whether man has become larger and stronger, or smaller and weaker, than his ancestors, we should, however bear in mind that an animal possessing great size, strength, and ferocity, and which, like the gorilla, could defend itself from all enemies, *would not perhaps have become social*; and this would most effectually have checked the acquirement of the higher mental qualities, such as sympathy and the love of his fellows".[27]

I am the Super-Force creating all matter which generates *all waves*. From all eternity, **I AM** the energy force that is; at all times **I AM** the source of all mass which

exists - - - a physical and potential presence - - - and My energy and mass generates the motions of *waves.*

These are three of My properties: my Force/ energy; My physical transitions; and My communicative waves/ spiritual inspiration. If your super-cooled quantum computers can calculate the probability of any event (dividing by prime numbers) and if they can store all of civilization's facts from the instant of creation in a small building, *do not doubt that I can use my Universe and it's super-cooled space to be aware of all existence at every moment.*

Soon, your Artificial Intelligence will express emotional responses to communications it receives. Do not doubt that I have the full capacity of all emotions

and that I am the source of all empathy and the reservoir of all mercy. You have been able to observe and measure only 4% of My creation. You call this *"ordinary matter"*. And yet you have calculated that 96% of what is affecting the acceleration of the universe - - - with *expansion* is what you call *"dark* /transparent *energy* (70%) - - - or with *contraction, "dark/* transparent *matter"* (26%). Can you not conceive of a loving *Super-Force existing beyond your capacity to measure?* You are like the honey bee unable to conceptualize that humans are capturing their laboriously produced honey and shipping it to England to sweeten their tea.

All your comprehension comes from the small organ atop your body - your brain. Can you not see that you are like your red blood cells coursing within my arteries - - attempting to understand why some arteries are blocked with atheromatous plaques or why you have caused your heart to stop by cascading into clots? Yet, **I am** *always aware* that all of my creation follows my laws of physics. From the moment of my Big Bang you can measure My cosmic microwave background radiation. You used to see the fluorescence on your old television screens when you would turn them on 70 years ago. Now you measure them to calculate your date of the universe's birth. **I am** your *waves of communication.* You have measured alpha, beta and gamma waves, muons and meson waves: *do not doubt I* have *waves of inspiration* which you have not yet been able to measure.

Scientists cannot explain or measure Me. Yet Albert Einstein, arguably the most brilliant scientist of all time, sensed there must be a "**Supreme Being**" to explain the mathematical certainty which allowed him to calculate the speed of light 100 years ago - - - and to deduce ingeniously his Special (& General) Theories of Relativity. Einstein is quoted as saying:

"My religion consists of a humble admiration of the illimitable spirit who reveals himself in the slight details we are able to perceive with our frail, feeble minds. That deeply emotional conviction of the presence of a superior reasoning power, which is revealed in the

192

incomprehensible universe, forms my idea of God." [4]

But accepting that *I do exist*, you might appropriately ponder why do *you* exist? Those of you who have become parents can surmise the urge to share the love for one another with **progeny.** Enjoy! Let me love you and share My Universe with you.

So Me, Myself, & I (Super-Force, Physical Presence & Waves of Inspiration) bursting with our love - have chosen to love and to *share all with you - - -* you are *the children of God* and **We** love all of you equally!

By now you have visualized the billions of galaxies in your universe with planets - both near and billions of light years away. **We** have hoped to share all of infinity with you for all eternity. It is your inheritance - - - but you must show yourself worthy of such a windfall. So what will you do to show you are worthy?

"*The Lord God then took the man and settled him in the* garden of Eden, to cultivate and care for it. The Lord God gave man this order: 'You are free to eat from any of the trees of the garden except the tree of knowledge of good and bad'." From that tree you shall not eat: the moment you eat from it you are surely doomed to die".

The Book of Wisdom expresses it this way:

"For God formed man to be imperishable; the image of his own nature he made him. But by the envy of the devil, death entered the world, and they who belong to his company experience it."

Somehow, even your most "primitive" ancestors realized that it would destroy your relationship with your Creator if you were to "know evil". This was the first acknowledgment of humankind that your Creator consisted of only *goodness*. And so you have been counseled by the prophet Amos:

"Seek good and not evil, that you may live; Then truly will the Lord, God of hosts, be with you as you claim! Hate evil and love good, and let justice prevail at the gate"

Yet besides My holiness, the prophet Isaiah taught you how to recognize my other qualities. Giving Me the attribute of maternal constancy in My love for you he says

"Can a woman forget her nursing child, and not have compassion on the son of her

womb? Surely, they may forget; Yet I would never forget you. See, I have inscribed you on the palm of My hands."

But no one has better revealed Me than My son, Jesus, when he told the story of the prodigal son:

"There was a man who had two sons. The younger said to his father, 'Give me my half of all the family property -all that would be mine after you die.' So the father divided everything he owned between his two sons. A few days later the younger son packed up all his things and left home to live in a faraway country. But he wasted all of his money living a wild life. After he had spent everything, there was a bad famine in that country and he became very hungry but could not buy any food. He went to work for a farmer who sent him out to feed the pigs. The young man was so hungry he could have eaten the food the pigs ate, but no one offered him even that. At last he came to his sense and said to himself, 'The people who work for my father have more than enough to eat and here I am starving to death. I will go back to my father and I will say to him: Father, I have sinned against God and against you: I am no longer good enough to be called your son. Treat me like one of your workers.'

So the young man started home. But while he was still a long way off, his father saw him coming and ran out to meet him. He took his son in his arms and kissed him. The young man said 'Father, I have sinned against God and against you. I am no longer good enough to be called your son.' But the father said to his servants, 'Quick! Bring out the best clothes, and put them on him. Put a ring on his finger and shoes on his feet. Get our best calf and prepare a feast. Let's eat and celebrate because my son was dead and he has come back to life. He was lost and has been found.'"

No one better interpreted the story of "The Prodigal Son" better than Henri J. M. Nouwen, interpreting Rembrandt's painting "The Return of the Prodigal Son".

"Father and Mother

Often I have asked friends to give me their first impression of Rembrandt's *Prodigal Son* . Inevitably, they point to the wise old man who forgives his son: the benevolent patriarch. The longer I looked at "the patriarch", the clearer it became to me that

Rembrandt had done something quite different from letting God pose as the wise old head of a family. It all began with *the hands*. The two are quite different. The father's left hand touching the son's shoulder is strong and muscular. The fingers are spread out and cover a large part of the prodigal's shoulder and back. I can see a certain pressure, especially in the thumb. That hand seems not only to touch, but, with its strength also to hold. Even though there is a gentleness in the way the father's left hand touches the son, it is not without a firm grip.

How different is the father' right hand! This hand does not hold or grasp. It is refined, soft, and very tender. The fingers are close to each other and they have an elegant quality. It lies gently upon the son's shoulder.

It wants to caress, to stroke, and to offer consolation and comfort. It is a mother's hand.

Some commentators have suggested that the masculine left hand is Rembrandt's own hand, while the right hand is similar to the right hand of *The Jewish Bride* painted in the same period. I like to believe that this is true." [28]

And so, from a revealing story told by Jesus, we get a glimpse of My tender "soft underbelly"- - - capable of showing a Father's strength and support, loving and forgiving, compassionate in our suffering; together with a maternal tenderness, solace and comforting. Jesus, Himself, described the intimate concern that I have towards you:

"Are not two sparrows sold for a small coin? Yet not one of them falls to the

ground without your Father's knowledge. Even the hairs of your head are counted. So do not be afraid; you are worth more than many sparrows."

Your early ancestors flailed at attempting to worship Me - - - offering burnt animals and oils or "first fruits". My prophet Micah tried to tell them what I wanted:

"O my people, what have I done to you, or how have I wearied you? Answer me! For I brought you up from the land of Egypt, from the place of slavery I released you; and I sent before you Moses, Aaron, and Miriam.

With what shall I come before the LORD, and bow before God most High? Shall I come before Him with burnt offerings, with calves a year old? Will the LORD be pleased with thousands of rams, with myriad streams of oil? Shall I give my first-born for my crime, the

201

fruit of my body for the sin of my soul? You have been told, O man, what is good and what the Lord requires of you: *Only to do the right and to love goodness and to walk humbly with your god*".

I AM all goodness and I ask that you strive your whole lives to choose goodness. Christ reminded you: "Be perfect as your heavenly father is perfect".

Yet, I am Aware that you have descended with beastly cravings and perfection is not for this Earth. If you fail in your quest for goodness, know that **I am** awaiting your remorse and the return to your senses, as the father in Christ's Prodigal Son story - - - and as Christ also has said to you:

"There will be more rejoicing in heaven over one sinner who repents than over ninety-nine righteous persons who do not need to repent."

EPILOGUE

Astrophysicist Ethan Siegel calculated that if the energy-mass at the moment of the "Big Bang" (some 13.65 billion years ago) contained just one *additional* proton weight, our universe would have collapsed upon itself "in its infancy". And, he continued, if it had contained just one *less* proton weight, it would have scattered into oblivion before even beginning to "grow its atoms" (let alone its stars and planets). [25]

You should therefore appreciate that our existence on this universe is no mere *"accident"*. Albert Einstein is quoted as saying: *"Coincidence is God's way of remaining anonymous"*.

Experimental quantum physicists and theoretical/ mathematical physicists offered differing explanations for *"How did the Universe come into existence?"* And if our existence in this universe is part of God's plan - just *what is this plan?* Why are we so *imperfect now?*

Deep within the center of each human brain lies a primitive "animal brain" (termed the "rhinencephalon" by neuroanatomists) which excites or "drives" us to aggression, territorial "grabbing"; provocative sexuality and recurrent hunger.

Sigmund Freud used his own psychoanalytic neologisms to call this part of "the *id*". Eric Byrne renamed it our "inner child" in his book **Games People Play**. We need not blame the devil for every raw and banal temptation to stray from the "straight and narrow" path. Although Christ did remind us that he saw "Satan fall like lightning from heaven".

Surrounding this animal basic inner core of brain nuclei is the product of 300,000 of years of competitive conquests and genetic selection of "the fittest"- - - the cerebral cortex of *homo sapiens*. These convolutions have not only given us the capacity to calculate that $E = m C^2$, but they have additionally imbued us with a conscience which forever reminds us that "It is wrong to murder, rape, or steal and plunder". Freud termed this part of the brain the "*super-ego*" and Byrne referred to it as our "inner parent".

Ever negotiating a truce in most of us between the "id" and the "super-ego" or the "child" and the "inner parent" is Freud's "*ego*" and Eric Byrne's the "inner adult" in us. Most of our lobes are processing the inner and outer worlds we encounter and we are seeking to construct a compromise between these conflicting elements - - - so that we may live our lives with inner peace.

Partly because we had not perfected this process of maintaining peacefulness even after the last 60,000 years of evolution; but partly because we required a role model for living our lives with purpose [especially God's purpose in creating us to enjoy immortality with Him in Paradise for all eternity] God devised an *incarnation: the only begotten son of God,* Jesus

Christ appeared around 2000 years ago to clarify the way to live our lives - giving us "the message" - the *truth* in life's confusing messages, and the (eternal) life in Paradise that can be ours - - - should we choose to accept it.

This book is an attempt to bring self-discovery to the reader - - - discovery of the basic truths which can be used to triumph over the basic instincts of humankind. Buddhists and Hindu "saints" are taught a philosophy of self-abnegation which would lead to an "ideal" state on Earth called *Nirvana* where the mind remains free of "wrong thoughts such as anger, lust or greed" and capable of accepting one's suffering with resignation. Jesus Christ came to teach us that we can enter a state of being which is beyond Nirvana. He called this state of existence "the kingdom of Heaven" . It is the *very realm of God, Himself.*

It has been difficult for the isolated and alienated soul to enter such a realm all by himself. The very concept of success has been the subject of world literature for over 2000 years. Aristotle and Plato sought formulas for the "good life, well lived" - - - "the Golden Mean" - - - or the "balanced life". Only in philosophy and only since the coming of Christ could it seriously be argued that "There is nothing new under the sun".

Nevertheless, the time-worn truths of existence are forever fresh when discovered by each of us today.

The Disney/Pixar empire created a comic hero in the "Toy Story" series. His name is Buzz Lightyear. Everyone laughs when he clicks his magic button to leap into hyper-speed as he shouts, "To infinity and beyond". But no one will be laughing when we catapult into the next phase of existence called "eternity" - - - which each of us must do someday.

Our philosophers since Dao De Jing wisely counsel us that a journey of a thousand miles begins with taking that "first step". It is my hope that these self-discovery chapters will help each of us prepare for that momentous transition to "Infinity & Beyond".

It is also my hope that everyone who reads this text will become convinced that he/she lives because *there is a God - Who set into being all that exists in the universe* at the time of the Big Bang- bursting with love to share the universe for eternity with us - his beloved children.

And because humankind evolved with such beastly drives to "rape, pillage, and plunder" - God devised the *Incarnation* (1) to show His profound love for us by sacrificing

His only begotten Son in atonement for humanity's sins; (2) that we might learn by

Christ's word and example how to enter God's realm; and (3) that by leaving us proof of His resurrection, we might be convinced that *we are immortal beings!*

And we must remember that "empty space" is *not empty.* It is filled with dark or transparent matter and energy - packed with subatomic particles such as *bosons* - and packed with "entangled twins of our subatomic consciousness" - **our entangled souls**?

Before there was a universe obeying Einstein's Theories of Relativity, most scientists claim that for microseconds after "the Big Bang", at the time of the Initial Singularity" (which is thought to have contained all the energy and Space-Time of the Universe), subatomic particles exploded *faster than the speed of light* in what they call "the Inflationary Epoch". [29]

These same scientists can generate "twin" particles and atoms today which can transfer information for our quantum computers, for example, (used in cryptography and for international financial transactions) and which transfer this information *faster than the speed of light* - i.e., immediately and simultaneously - no matter how far the "twins" are located. Recall, the Nobel Prize in Physics last year went to the scientists who proved this *experimentally!* This quantum process is called *entanglement.* *Entanglement means t*hat measurement of "Twin A" which might carry its data at an "upward spin", *simultaneosly and immediately* will measure the same data on "Twin B" - whose only difference would be its "downward

213

spin" - and which theoretically could be at *the opposite end of the universe!*

This information is carried by a process called *teleportation.* The transfer of information is immediate - thus "faster than the speed of light" - even if Twin B is located at the other end of the universe (which, although expanding infinitely is at the present 270,000,000,000,000,000,000,000 miles away now). [Light travels at 671 miles per hour so travel by light speed would take almost 46 years!]

It's such a huge universe, my twin consciousness wouldn't want to travel in a SpaceX "Starship", or Sierra Nevada's "Dream Chaser", or Boeing's "Starliner", or even Jeff Bezo's (Blue Origin) "Artemis". They are all too slow. No! Teleportation is the only way to travel. "Beam me up, Scotty!" as Captain Kirk used to say in the Star Trek series. [Of course, whole bodies like William Shatner's can't really teleport]. But real images and real communication has been teleporting to the "twin consciousness" particles since humankind first walked this Earth. [Some day, at the "end of the ages", Jesus promised an actual resurrection of our bodies. [We might look forward to that because we're "kind of attached to our bodies"]. Until then, don't belittle the fact that you might have a twin consciousness "out there in the universe" that can instantaneously know everything that happens to you on Earth. Yet, although your "twin memories" will be enhanced, possibly with much greater clarity for past and present - (because of the absence of neurohormones possibly) - there seems to be *no experience of suffering or pain* "out there in space" - *if we can believe the REDs.*

Near Death Experiences have been noted since antiquity. Helena Carol, Ph.D, scientific coordinator of Neurological Rehabilitation Center of the University Hospital in Liege, Belgium says up to 23% of survivors of cardiac arrest patients have reported these Near Death Experiences. At the time of His death from crucifixion, Jesus promised the "good thief":

"This day, you will be with me in Paradise!"

Perhaps he was referring to the "twin consciousness"/ soul of the good thief, in outer space: a reference to our *immortal, entangled soul!*

REFERENCES:

1. Parnia, Sam; et al.; "Guidelines and Standards for the Study of Death - a Multidisciplinary Consensus Statement and Proposed Future Directions"; Annals of the New York Academy of Sciences, Vol. 1511, Issue 1; pages1-261, May 2022, Wiley.

2. Kerskens, Christian Matthias; Lopez, David; SCI NEWS, Oct 20, 2022. "Experimental indications of non-classical brain functions"; *J. PHYS. COMMUN 6, 103001; DOI;10.1088/2399-65-6528/AC94BE.*

3. Spitzer, Robert; "Near Death Experiences Pt. 2"; **You Tube**; July 4, 2023.

4. *Ibid.*

5. Kubler-Ross, Elizabeth; Kessler, David; **On Grief & Grieving**; Scribner; 2005; ISBN 978-1-4767-7555-5

6. Siegel, Ethan; Starts With A Bang; "This is Why Our Universe Didn't Collapse Into A Black Hole"; **Starts With A Bang**; https://www.forbes.com>startswithabang> 2018/03/23

7. https://www.sutori.com/en/story/big-bang-the-first-second-dxq8TdM5gRqLXcqHNaop

8. Hawking, Stephen W, (1988) A Brief History of Time, New York, Bantam, Dell Publishing Group ISBN 978&0&553&10953&5

9. Focus: Nobel Prize - "Why Particles Have Mass"; October 11, 2013, *Physics* 6, 111

10. Measurement of the Higgs boson mass from the H->YY and H->ZZ; http://cds.cern.ch/record/1709081

11. **Precise measurement of the Higgs boson mass**; 3 July 2014 By ATLAS Collaboration; https://atlas.cern//updates/briefing/precise-measurement-higgs-boson-mass

12. **Measurement of the Higgs boson mass from the H->YY and H->ZZ : http://cds.cern.ch/record/1709081**

13. https://www.scientificamerican.com>article>higgs-boson; June 26, 2014

14. https://iopscience.iop.org>articla>012015>pdf Measurement of the Higgs Boson

15. Barnett, Lincoln; **The Universe & Dr. Einstein**, 1957, Time, Inc.

16. Lewis, C.S.; **Mere Christianity**; Harper One; ISBN 978-0-065292-0
217. 14 Shroud of Turin Research Project; 1978; You Tube

18. Rogers, Raymond N.; "Studies on the Radiocarbon Sample From the Shroud of Turin"; thermochemica.acta; accepted 12 September 2004; published 2005

19. The ENEA Study (http:www.lastampa.it.2011/12vaticaninsider/eng/.inquiries-and-interviews/theshroud-is-not-a-fake-jdiKEyI)uDsE4XpV13TeK/.

20. Whanger, Alan D. & Mary; "Polarized Image Overlay Technique"; Applied Optics; Vol. 24, No. 6, 15 March 1985.

21. Spitzer, Fr. Robert, S.J., "Science & The Shroud of Turin"; Napa Institute Conference, 2017; You Tube

22. Lederman, Leon Nobel Laureate; Hill, Christopher, **Beyond the God Particle**; 2013, Prometheus Books; Amherst, New York, 14228-2119

23. Tyson, Neil de Grasse, **Astrophysics for People in a Hurry**; 2017; W.W. Norton & Company, London.

24. Choi, Charles Q., "Our Expanding Universe; Age, History & Other Facts; SPACE.COM, June 16, 2017

25. Siegel, Ethan; "This is Why Our Universe Didn't Collapse Into A Black Hole; **Starts With A Bang**; https://www.forbes.com>startswithabang>2018/03/23

26. Rovelli, Carlo; **The Order of Time**; p. 54; 2018; Riverhead Books; New York

27. Darwin, Charles; **The Descent of Man**; Great Books of the Western World; Vol. 49; Encyclopedia Brittanica; 1952; London.

28. Nouwen, Henri J.M.; **The Return of the Prodigal Son**; "A Story of Homecoming"; DoubleDay Image Books; New York; 1992

29. https://en.wikipedia.org>Initial_Singularity - 2021

BIBLIOGRAPHY:

1. Rees, Martin, Corte, Maria; "Our Place in the Universe"; **Scientific American**, September 2020.

2. Cloninger, C. Robert M.D., Przybeck, Thomas R., Ph.D.; Svrakic, Dragan M. Ph.D., Dept. Of Psychiatry, Washington University School of Medicine; **The Tridimensional Personality Questionnaire**; U.S. Normative data; see **Archives of General Psychiatry**, Dec. 1, 1993; pp 975-990.

3. talentsmart.com/888.888.SMART

4. 14th Dalai Llama; Tutu, Archbishop Desmond; **The Book of Joy**; 2016; Cornerstone Publishers; UK

5. Benvenuti, James MD; **Normal Minds**; 2016; Angeli Press

6. Larson, Rick; DVD; **The Star of Bethlehem**, 2007

7. Mother Teresa; Ligurian, Nov 1997; reprinted from "Mother Teresa in My Own Words"; Liguori Publications, p. 72

8. Spitzer, Fr. Robert, S.J., "Science & The Shroud of Turin"; Napa Institute Conference, 2017; You Tube